Spirit-led

Parenting

From Fear to Freedom in Baby's First Year

Copyright Notice

Spirit-led

Parenting

From Fear to Freedom in Baby's First Year

By Laura Oyer and Megan Tietz

Dedication

To our children, for giving us the courage to find a new path

To our husbands, for walking hand-in-hand with us along the way

Contents

What Others Are Saying

"Confession: I intended to comment thoughtfully about this book as a fellow writer. But then I put my five month old baby boy to bed, settled into the pages, and couldn't put them down. I intended to get an overview and dash off some affirming words. Instead, I read and read, and I connected as a mother--I felt like I'd made friends across the pages. Buy this for the new moms in your life, so that on the longest, most sleepless, most desperate nights of baby life, they'll feel like they have two helpful, wise friends in Megan and Laura. What better gift than that?"

Shauna Niequist, author of *Cold Tangerines* & *Bittersweet*

~~

"Becoming a mom or dad is scary. One way to address those fears is by consuming parenting books full of rules, tips, and techniques. But the truth is, your child isn't reading those books and doesn't care what those authorities say. A better, saner idea is to parent with the grace, sensitivity, and individuality each kid needs. That's the powerful message of *Spirit-Led Parenting*, and it's one every mom or dad needs to hear."

Jason Boyett, author of *O Me of Little Faith: True Confessions of a Spiritual Weakling*

~~

"Where most books admonish parents to tightly control their babies' schedules and protect their own lives from changing, Laura Oyer and Megan Tietz encourage us instead to heed Scripture's call to cultivate a servant's heart in our approach to parenthood. They offer moms and dads relief from the fears that so often drive their parenting decisions, and exhort them to rediscover the nurturing instincts that God has given them but that society and culture try to silence. *Spirit-Led Parenting* should be on every expectant mother's nightstand, regardless of how many children she already has. It is a treasure of wisdom that is sure to make the first year of a child's life much more enjoyable for mom, dad, and baby."

Alison Strobel/Ali Morrow, author of novels for women and storybooks for children

~~

"Ever had that nagging fear that you're gonna screw your kids up for life? Thank Jesus for Megan and Laura and their sweet, comforting, Scripture-inspired words of freedom. *Spirit-Led Parenting* is like a great big ol' sigh of peace for your soul."

Marla Taviano, author of *From Blushing Bride to Wedded Wife, Changing Your World One Diaper at a Time,* and *Expecting: Praying for Your Child's Development – Body and Soul*

~~

"As a recovering perfectionist who held herself to unattainable standards with her firstborn, I can shout from the rooftops with affirmation that Megan and Laura have given moms a GIFT. The words in this book are seasoned with friendship, grace, and freedom; reading it was like drinking coffee with girlfriends who get me. Their message is too good to not share with moms of babies everywhere: God has given you everything you need to be the right mom for your baby. He is a God that lavishly gifts us with redemptive freedom. Why would it not be so with parenting? I am thankful that these women wrote these words and then shared them with the rest of us."

Tsh Oxenreider, founder of SimpleMom.net and author of *Organized Simplicity* and *One Bite at a Time*

~~

"*Spirit-Led* Parenting speaks to the new moms of a new generation who in all other areas are open to thinking outside the box and pushing the boundaries of life, but might have gotten tripped up by claims that there is only one right way to parent. As *Spirit-Led Parenting* shares personal testimonies of the authors and other parents it encourages seeking the Lord to find the solutions to the common challenges of parenting that are individual and provided by the Holy Spirit. God gave you this baby, and that means He believes you are able to be the mother this baby needs. This book will encourage you to step out in faith and be the best mother for your baby."

Crystal Lutton, author of *Biblical Parenting*

~~

"*Spirit-Led Parenting: From Fear to Freedom in Baby's First Year* is a beautiful, honest book rooted in the idea that living well with children calls for faith above facts or rules. Expectant moms, new moms, and even veteran moms will discover a deeper understanding of God, the Perfect Parent, and His plan for their family. Filled with practical advice on everything from breastfeeding to parenting as a couple, Spirit-Led Parenting also includes personal stories from both the authors and other parents. Opening this book means opening yourself to a new way of parenting, and raising children transforms into a grace-filled encounter where fear, guilt, and doubts are replaced with love, hope, and the freedom to nurture your children as God intended.

Kate Wicker , wife, mom of littles, journalist, & expert in hazardous waste removal. Author of *Weightless: Making Peace With Your Body* and KateWicker.com

~~

"I was completely drawn in by Megan and Laura's words in *Spirit-Led Parenting*. I cried my way through the first chapter, recalling the regret and guilt I experienced through my first days and weeks as a mama. I wish I would have had this book to lean on then. Thrilled to know that new moms will have this guide enabling them to enter motherhood along a path of freedom instead of fear and frustration. "

Jamie Martin, founder of SteadyMom.com and author of *Steady Days* and *Mindset for Moms*

~~

"Thank you, Megan and Laura! I have been waiting for a book like this for years! I can hand it out to new parents with absolute confidence that they will receive soul food, grace and wholeness, love and gentleness as they embark on their parenting journey. (I'll be buying them in bulk, no doubt, and it will be every baby shower gift from here on out.) In a church culture that can so often emphasize control and fear-based "what-if" scenarios for exacting obedience even from the start of our parenting journey, it is so refreshing to read that parenting is not a war, there is no "us vs. them" with our children. Our example in all things is this: I want to parent my tinies the way that God parents me. There is no recipe or training guide for marionettes of perfect obedience but instead a long process of capturing hearts, pointing towards Jesus. And the incredible thing about this heart-attitude for parenting is that it transforms our own hearts, minds and lives to be more like our Savior. This is a beautifully written book by two mothers whose voice I have learned to trust."

Sarah Bessey, writer, blogger, non-profit marketing director and mother of three tinies

~~

"As a soon-to-be-mother, *Spirit Led Parenting* eased the fears I had over what's expected for new parents. With incredible grace, Megan and Laura remind us of what's important: leaning on the One who knows what's best for our family. I recommend this book to anyone who struggles with living up to the status quo and knows there's something more - something better for their children."

Elora Nicole Ramirez, author of *Come Alive* and *when Beauty Pursues You*, eloranicole.com

~~

"I was never much for parenting books because I felt they demanded from me an adherence to methods of which I was never entirely convinced. What a gift, that *Spirit-Led Parenting* offers a better way: relationship over rules, grace over guidelines, freedom over fear. This book makes no haughty demands; rather, it humbly points us to our great Parent and asks only that we follow."

Tamara Lunardo, editor, *What a Woman is Worth* (forthcoming, Civitas Press), contributor, *Not Alone: Stories of Living with Depression* (Civitas Press), writer, TamaraOutLoud.com and DeeperStory.com, mother of five

~~

"Oh how I wish that *Spirit-Led Parenting* had been in my hands those first few weeks of my son's life. I just knew I was a failure because all my attempts at breastfeeding were failing. This book is a breath of fresh air and a must-read for all new parents. Let's let go of the guilt and embrace parenting that isn't one-size-fits-all."

Emily Carter, writer at The Pilot's Wife (http://thepilotswifeblog.com/)

~~

"Through their words in *Spirit-Led Parenting: From Fear to Freedom in Baby's First Year*, Megan and Laura invite readers to find their path to freedom as a parent and a spouse. From fantastic stories to soul-moving words, they share the beautiful Jesus-inspired concept that if we give grace (to ourselves, our children and each other) we are set free to parent in the way God uniquely created our children to crave. No longer will we have to "chase perfection" as parents, we now have practical and heart-strengthening skills to follow the path that we were created to walk. This book covers topics most parenting books avoid, while still bringing fresh perspective to the age old questions of what to do about baby sleeping/feeding/crying. A fantastic addition to even the most seasoned parent's home library!"

Arianne Segerman, freelance writer at www.tothinkistocreate.com and mom of four

~~

"This is a message that desperately needs to be shared with the body of Christ. Deeply spiritual, deeply personal, these two mothers help illuminate the Spirit-Led path to parenting. It reads like a breath of fresh air, like sharing a cup of coffee with a friend. Its words of comfort and peace will help calm the fears and anxieties of the parenting journey and light the way to freedom."

Leslie Freeman, author RealChildDevelopment.com, and founder of The Refuge

~~

"I have perused the pages of *Spirit Led Parenting* while awaiting the arrival of my third baby and have wished, with each page turn, that I had read these words before I held my first child six years ago. Instead of anxiousness, fear, and formulas, Megan and Laura use their stories to pour upon new mothers grace and gentleness. In a world full of prescriptions for perfect parenting, these women show God's methods to be peaceful and individual while beautifully looking at how He leads and holds the hearts of mothers, fathers and their precious little ones."

Ashleigh Baker, writer at ashleighbaker.net

Laura's Acknowledgements

My Father God, Christ my Savior, and the Spirit that led me to freedom. All other ground is sinking sand.

Mark — The love of my life and my partner in parenting. Thank you for believing I could do this and for turning a blind eye to housework even more sorely neglected than usual. Also, for being an unceasingly sensible parent. Our children really needed at least one. I love you madly.

Maya and Noah — Always my babies. You constantly expand my heart and teach me far more than I could ever teach you. May you grow to trust His voice and leading above all else. And to forget all of the times you saw me turn to Starbucks therapy. Your Mama loves you to the moon and back.

Our parents and families for their support and cheerleading. And friends who amaze me. Nichole, for your encouragement and miraculous photography skills. Rhoda and Amber for lattes and bread. Melissa and Maria for wonderful read-through input. Rach and the women of my small groups (Ryann, Emily, Jen, Myriah, Gretchen, Lori, Dorothy, Alice, Amber B.) for praying and listening to me ramble on. I'm so thankful for you.

Our beloved January '05 Mamas, and the communities at SortaCrunchy and In the Backyard, who lent wisdom and stories and motivated us to keep writing. This dream began and grew in the hearts of many.

Jonathan— Our partner and mentor at Civitas Press. Thank you for believing in two moms with a message, and in the potential of what that message could be. Your guidance and encouragement to work hard — and then harder — has made all the difference.

Megan—My mind-twin and heart sister. I am a better mother, writer, and person for having walked this journey with you. Not only does your incredible talent inspire me, but your generosity and gracious spirit never cease to amaze. Your friendship is such a treasure to me.

Myron & Dana—What you mean in my life could fill another book, and this one wouldn't have been possible without your influence. Thank you for your guidance and friendship, for always pointing me to God, for knowing me well enough to call me on my shortcomings and faithfully believing in me in spite of them. And most of all, for modeling Spirit-led parenting in my life. I love you so much.

Megan's Acknowledgements

To all of the January 2005 moms who have shared in our story from day one, thank you for allowing us to be a place of confession and celebration. Were it not for our gathering place, this book would never have been born.

To the community at Gentle Christian Mothers, thank you for tireless advocacy for gospel-centered parenting. Thank you for mentoring me and so many others, and thank you for reminding me time and again of the need for this message.

To the community of readers at SortaCrunchy and In the Backyard, where could I begin to say thank you? Your support, your prayers, your comments, your emails, your presence ... it is all priceless to me. Thank you for joining us in the journey.

To Jonathan, our incredible editor, thank you for taking a chance on us. Thank you for hearing our passion and helping us bring the message to life.

To Laura, my always-and-forever mind twin, thank you for holding my hand and holding me to deadlines and holding me up. You are the best.

To my confidants on the other side of screens across the world: Missy, Marla, Kelly, Sarah, Nish, Ashleigh, Arianne, Jill and my OBG Tribe. Thank you for being my safe place. To my more-real-than-real community of support of the 3-D variety: Andy, Jaime,

Laura, Toni, Libby, Raylee, and Courtney. Thank you for cheering me on, lifting me up, speaking the truth, and caring for our family.

To Todd, Mindy, Brandon, Robin, and Sarah, thank you for sharing family life with us. To Emily, there are not enough words to ever adequately say thank you; you were cheerleading this book long before I dared to dream it could be. To my parents and parents-in-law, thank you for shepherding us in the ways of Christ.

To my husband, Kyle, thank you for believing in me even when I am sobbing at my desk. Thank you for never failing me, even when I have failed you. You are my favorite.

To our girls, thank you for inspiring me, in everything and in every way.

My Father God, my Lord Jesus, my Indwelling Spirit, words fail me. *It is for freedom we have been set free.* May I never lose the wonder of it all.

Preface

Hospital beds. Monitors. Nameless nurses. Absent doctor. Long labor. Epidural. Forceps. Fluid in lungs. Taking away my baby. My first experience with birth was anything but natural. It seemed like a Mad Hatter ride through Wonderland with twists and turns and no end in sight. I had nothing to compare my experience against, so I just held on tight and hoped for the best. But I knew in my spirit that this was not as it should be. Not as God intended this miracle of life-giving to be.

But then they finally brought my baby to me, and laid her on my chest. And from that moment that I held my first baby in my arms for the first time, I knew she was a gift of God. I looked into her bright blue eyes, marveled at her long eyelashes, and smiled at the tiny little mouth that was curved into a smile just for me. I knew at that moment that being a mother was a gift of God. I knew instinctively that this new and beautiful life was mine not just to feed and clothe, but to form and fill with my love. Despite the unnatural beginnings of my wild ride through giving birth, I knew in my spirit my first child's birth was giving me something—the natural, God-given impulse to be a mother to my child.

I thought the chorus of voices telling me what to do, when, and how at the hospital would fade when I took my baby home. They did not. As I eagerly entered the daily life of new motherhood, I soon found myself surrounded by new voices. They were telling me what was the best way, even God's way, to take care of my infant child, and if I didn't listen to them I could harm my baby by what I did or didn't do. They offered exacting rules and schedules for how to feed her, care for her, nurse her, put her to bed, discipline her, and on and on. They were certainly well-meaning and often godly advisors, but it seemed like each had an answer for every question and questioned every answer that was not their way. If the voices were supposed to make me feel more confident, they didn't. They too often created confusion and even fear. I began to feel an emotional weight from the shackles of guilt and performance that threatened to restrict me from listening to my own motherly instincts. It was not natural.

At that point, I made a decision. Rather than trusting the methods of experts, who more often than not disagreed with one another, I decided to trust the Spirit of God to guide me as a mother. If I could trust God for wisdom and direction in every other area of my life, it seemed biblical and right that I should be able to trust him to help me be a good mother. After all, motherhood was in the heart of God at creation, so it is not a mystery but part of his natural created order for life. And since the Spirit of God lives in me as a helper, motherhood should easily qualify for his help.

As I began to actively believe that God would be active in my motherhood, I found a new and liberating freedom in the desire to become a mother after God's heart. It was not about which expert's formula for motherhood was best, but about an average mom living by faith in the God who designed me to be a mother with his Spirit living in me. That has been the paradigm of my parenting ever since. It is the heart of all my books on motherhood, and the passion that has driven me in my ministry for two decades to help restore moms' hearts to God's heart for motherhood.

Spirit-Led Parenting: From Fear to Freedom in Baby's First Year captures the heart of what I was feeling and experiencing as a new mother, and what my heart was telling me was natural and right. Laura and Megan give a seasoned voice to a way of thinking about how to be a mother to a newborn and infant that does not ask you to be dependent on them, but encourages you to trust the God who lives in you, loves you, and loves your baby. They listened to voices that set them free to be the mothers God designed them to be, and have shared the results of their search for natural, heartfelt motherhood in this book. You will not find guilt in this wonderful book, but grace, beauty, and joy that is the natural and normal expectation of motherhood. You will find freedom.

My prayer is that mothers with newborns and infants will read this book and be set free from the often onerous rules and expectations of the many voices out there in the marketplace of ideas vying for their mom hearts. Motherhood is a joyful and beautiful experience designed by God before the fall and given the divine seal of approval as "good." It is a blessing, not a burden. Laura and Megan are wonderfully gentle guides into the freedom that God intended moms to experience when they hold the precious gift he has entrusted to them, their babies, in their arms.

If you are a new mom, or a veteran mom about to give birth again, you have opened the right book. You only get one chance to give your baby a wonderful first year of life. This book will set you free to enjoy that first year of motherhood with all the blessings, grace, and delight that God intends you to experience. Naturally, that's the way it should be.

Sally Clarkson

ITakeJoy.com, MomHeart.org, Mom Heart Ministry

Author of *The Mission of Motherhood* , *The Ministry of Motherhood*, *The Mom Walk*, and *Seasons of a Mother's Heart*

Introduction

I wish someone had told me...

If only I had known...

Those statements, sprinkled throughout heartfelt conversations between two friends, were the inspiration that led to the book in your hands.

When God crossed our paths, we discovered in each other a shared history — a journey into motherhood that mirrored our own, along with an intense call to speak the message that God wrote on each of our hearts and pulled together as two parts of a whole.

As you will soon read, it was parenting books which fueled the anxiety in each of our hearts as we began our journeys as mothers. While we are confident and passionate about the words God has asked us to share in the chapters to come, we want you to know that we recognize the responsibility they carry.

Our intent in putting our experiences and philosophy to paper is not to suggest that there is one "right" way that every parent must care for a baby. In fact, it is that exact assertion that we each felt coming our way from the mainstream school of thought that, in turn, led us to present another way to parent from a Christian perspective. It is our prayer that this book may help other new parents who are entering this dizzying new stage of life wanting desperately to honor God, preserve their marriages, and raise well-adjusted children, to recognize that there is more than one way to do those things—and that the Lord is faithful to lead you to the right way for your family.

It is also not our intent to imply that we have this all figured out, by any stretch of the imagination! We frequently find ourselves in moments where our desire to mother from a Spirit-led perspective is severely challenged. It's far easier to write calmly about these matters when the sun is shining, the toddler is sleeping, and the six-year-old is happily playing on her own. It's much more difficult to keep perspective when you're trapped inside on a rainy day with an exhausted infant in the woes of teething, and you are so tired that you can't remember your own birthday.

We fail many times, and will countless more, to embody the spirit of parenting that we so deeply desire to live out. Yet through it all, we have both found that even as we've added new babies— with all-new personalities and challenges—to our families, and as we're stretched farther than ever before, our deeply-held belief in the concept of parenting led by the Spirit remains the same. We truly believe that this philosophy has changed our lives, blessed our children, and strengthened our marriages. And we believe it is one that is supported by Scripture and mirrors the example of parenthood we find in the Bible of God as Father, as well as in Christ's model of how to live in relationship with other people.

With a deep breath and open hands, we offer our stories and lessons learned as praise-filled testimony of what God has done in our lives, in the prayerful hope that He might use our words to spark a movement among new parents—one that finds freedom in following His lead.

Section One

If only it were so easy.

If only you held the answer to your every question about parenting a baby in your hands right now.

If only anyone could give you all the answers you need.

Books on parenting fill the shelves of bookstores of brick and bookstores of mouse clicks. We believed what we read in the pages, that the advice of man could give us all we needed to know. That belief came with a great cost, and the price tag was peace.

When we bought into the message that there was *one* right way to parent a baby, we didn't know we were also buying its unshakeable companion: Fear.

But as our stories unfolded, the One who has wisdom to answer every question introduced us to the one thing we were so terrified to embrace but so desperate to know: Freedom.

We want to begin by telling you our story, inviting you to hear how gently the Spirit led us from fear to freedom. Our heart's desire is for you to learn from our tear-shedding, hair-pulling, hopelessly-crying journey, so that you might avoid a little of the pain we endured. This is the unvarnished truth, and you'll find it all to be quite messy. From that mess, God has redeemed a message that we'll spend the rest of our lives declaring as truth: *there is another way.*

Chapter One

As We Began

May 2004 changed *everything* in *every way* for two women in the heartland.

That was the month that trembling hands held positive pregnancy tests alongside hopes and dreams for the future. In Indiana, it was Laura who first discovered that she and her husband's lives would be forever changed when those little lines turned pink. Days later and miles away in Texas, the story of Megan's family turned the page into a brand new chapter.

Laura and Megan had never met, but their paths were already beautifully entangled. The passage of time and the wonders of online community would eventually cause them to realize that January 2005 delivered healthy and beautiful baby girls to both of them, but it was the months that followed that would baptize them with fire and ordain them to speak a powerful message to new parents everywhere.

-Megan's Story-

Click.

The latch caught as I closed the door to my infant daughter's bedroom, and my breath caught in my throat. I closed my eyes and counted …

One.

Two.

Three.

I didn't make it to five before a bellowing wail from her tiny body filled my ears. I slid against the door down to the floor as my own tears splashed hot against my cheeks. My fists clenched tight in my lap as my heart raced and my cheeks burned. I knew — *I knew* — if I would go in and pick her up and rock her to sleep, she would be fine. But with every heartbeat that thumped in my ears, I heard the voice of the experts:

> *Don't use negative sleep props.*
>
> *Start as you mean to go on.*
>
> *Let baby learn independence.*
>
> *Don't be in bondage to baby's needs.*
>
> *Temporary crying is better than long-term sleep problems.*

I pounded my fists against my forehead and sobbed. Why? Why could she not sleep the way the books said she should sleep? Worse yet, why didn't I have the strength — the inner resolve — to let her cry? For three months, I had awakened each day with a pit in my stomach. For three months, nothing about life with a new baby was remotely close to what I had imagined. For three months, I felt like each new day was just another day to do battle with my newborn. I was the parent, and if I was going to do things the right way, the godly way, I had to win.

Right?

I'm an oldest child, an honor student, and a lifelong perfectionist. My husband and I had been married for over six years before we became parents, which is plenty of time to meticulously curate lists of "Our Children Will Never ... " Before our first child was born, a book fell into my hands along with some wonderful words of advice. I ignored the advice (more on that later) and devoured the book. The book offered structure! The book offered common sense! The book offered a perfect, peaceful existence with a new baby! The spoken advice merely offered freedom. As it turned out, I didn't want freedom. I wanted someone to tell me what to do. I had waited a long time for a baby, and I was not going to mess this up.

And so with the book's hearty encouragement and solid instructions, I developed a plan. My daughter and I, we would glide through our days and people would comment on how easy, how delightful, how perfect my baby was. I nearly waltzed into the hospital, so confident was I in the idea that I had this thing under control.

But then everything suddenly shifted out of control. Though my labor began with a great start, by the time I reached seven cm of dilation, complications began to develop and the growing concern of both the nurses and my doctor were alarming. In the blink of an eye, I was on my hands and knees on a hospital gurney, nearly taking corners on two wheels as we made our way to the operating room. The air in the OR was thick with tension and I quietly cried while my terrified husband whispered in my ear. Finally, far too long after she had been delivered, we heard her meek cry.

I don't think I was able to fully breathe again until we were tucked into our post-partum room. As soon as I was able to, I snuggled my new baby—Dacey Allyse—close to me while I thanked God over and over again for saving her life. Our hospital maintained a 100% room-in approach for mothers and new babies, but I didn't need a hospital policy to persuade me to never let her out of my sight.

No book on parenting even came close to capturing the immediate, fierce, and intense bond I felt with my new baby. By the end of the first night, I had pulled Dacey into bed with me and already I felt guilt for breaking one of "the rules."

The first two weeks at home were blissful. As both of us worked through the many pain management drugs in our systems from our emergency C-section delivery, I was able to dreamily rest as she slept peacefully in the Moses basket on the floor beside me. After two weeks had passed, however, she woke up to the world and it became very clear very quickly that our life would look nothing like the organized, orderly, controlled lives of the model parents in the book.

Disillusionment and despair quickly replaced the euphoria of new parenthood. Every nighttime wake-up, every too-short nap, every time I rocked her to sleep, I was confronted with my failure. Friends who had long-since lived through the newborn phase offered encouragement in how to make it through the crying that ensued each time I tried to lay her down to go to sleep on her own. I dutifully tried each suggestion: taking a shower so I couldn't hear her crying, turning off the baby monitor, wedging a towel under her bedroom door.

I just could not do it.

I rescued her every time.

And so I found myself slumped against her bedroom door, sobbing as she sobbed, asking myself for the millionth time what was wrong with my baby, and berating myself for giving in again. I went into her room, lowered the crib rail, and gathered her into my arms. As we settled into the comfort of the rocking chair, both of us gasping and sniffling, I leaned my head back, closed my eyes and prayed, *"God, isn't there another way?"*

-Laura's Story-

The digital display switched silently from 5:59 to 6:00, ushering in the time of morning that should carry a sense of peace and calm, hope brimming at the promise of another day. I sat on the couch, wide awake and anxiously biting my lip as I mentally checked off another night of total parenting failure.

Drifting off to sleep in my arms was my beautiful baby girl. Maya was our first child, and my husband, Mark, and I were completely in love with her. Healthy, beautiful, and growing more pudgy and playful by the day, Maya seemed to be thriving. Still, this morning my heart could not focus on the positives, preoccupied instead with the questions that loomed constantly in recent days:

Why is she waking up so much? Why is she eating so often? This can't be normal ... can it? **What is wrong with my baby?**

Why can't I follow directions? Why can't I just do what the books say? Am I just not strong enough to be a good mother? **What is wrong with me?**

If I can't gain control over my instincts (which are clearly defective), am I not only failing in my parenting ... but failing spiritually as well? **Am I turning my back on God?**

For as long as I can remember, I've thrived on clear direction from others. Products that arrive lacking obvious, step-by-step instructions make me crazy. My nightmare assignments in high school were those that were open-ended, and I can distinctly remember standing beside the desk of my biology teacher, asking questions meant to trick him into helping me outline one such project.

"Laura, the point of this assignment is for you to come up with your own ideas," he gently reminded me.

"I know," was my defeated answer, "But I was kind of hoping you'd just tell me what to do."

My independent spirit was inspiring, was it not? Just call me Erin Brockovich.

It's not that I was a complete pushover. It's just that I often assumed that someone else knew better than I did and had the answers all figured out. While I love to cook, I went for years without ever making adjustments to recipes, because I figured that the person who first concocted the dish had perfected the process. When planning my wedding, I often deferred to the ideas of our parents or attendants about what would make an enjoyable experience for the guests, because what did I really know about planning a wedding, anyway?

As I grew into a relationship with God in my teen years, I began to pray for direction on matters big and small, and since then I've received some messages that I could embrace with a measure of confidence. But you know those times when God doesn't give a completely transparent answer right away? I am not a fan of that. It is said that God often speaks in whispers, but I'd prefer that His voice consistently carry at the same decibel level as a cable news program. *Lord, could you please scream at me in such a way that I cannot possibly doubt what You think?* He doesn't often oblige that mature request. And so for most my life, I haven't truly trusted myself to discern His whispers among the other voices in those situations ... I've mostly just listened to the one that speaks loudest. *Someone just give me the answer.*

In many ways, the story of my entry into parenthood mirrors Megan's. The moment I stood in the bathroom gazing at two pink lines, I immediately dashed to the kitchen to pour my precious stockpile of Diet Coke down the drain. I wanted to protect my tiny baby who I just knew was already addicted to caffeine and disfigured by aspartame. I was bound and determined to figure out the right way to be a mother. And thankfully, as anyone who's ever announced a pregnancy has discovered, there is no shortage of advice to be found on the subject.

Mark and I were inundated with information on the best way — even God's way — to raise an infant. Several people introduced me to the same book that Megan received and I, too, was completely enchanted with the promises contained within its pages. Taking careful mental notes, I breathed great relief, thankful for this voice that was loud and clear within my social circles and was offering me the answers to parental success. I now knew exactly what to do — and just as importantly, what not to do — to achieve a harmonious home, raise an obedient child, and order our lives in a way that pleased God.

And then Maya was born. Eight pounds of sweetness, from her wide, soulful eyes to the thick, dark hair that would take months to relax from spikes and swoops into a smooth, manageable style. Little did I know, as I cradled her in the hospital that first night, that her personality would mirror that hair in many ways and that my careful plans to follow the advice of the "experts" would crumble around me almost immediately.

Right from the start, there were some struggles we hadn't counted on. Breastfeeding was far more difficult than expected and required hours of assistance from lactation consultants and products that would aid in overcoming Maya's latch issues. Once she was eating more easily, she didn't want to stop, and I was feeding her

every hour-and-a-half almost round-the-clock. I was exhausted —
physically, mentally, and emotionally. It was only my husband's
support and God's faithfulness in sustaining my strength that got
me through the early weeks.

Now she was three months old, and in many ways we had begun
to adjust. Those brown eyes crinkled up at the corners as we were
regularly greeted by her toothless grins. Breastfeeding, while still
a struggle, was something that I no longer faced with complete
trepidation. I was even beginning to adjust to the sleep-deprivation
and constant laundry piles. Even so, I wrestled with heavy guilt and
gnawing fear. And every question from well-meaning friends —
excellent parents whom I longed to emulate — would drive the
shame deeper.

*"Oh, she's three months old ... so she's probably eating every four hours
now. That's such a relief isn't it?"*

We weren't on a feeding schedule. I'd mumble through an evasive
response, then return home to resume our all-day-long nursing
frenzy.

*"Is she sleeping through the night yet?" they'd ask, expectantly. "How's
sleep training going?"*

No, she wasn't sleeping through the night. Not nearly. And ... oh
yes, sleep training. That book. The one whose every word I'd hung
on just months before. The one that offered such clear answers.
Laura-the-student would have jumped at the sight of step-by-step
solutions. Laura-the-beginning-cook would have followed the
recipe to the teaspoon. Laura-the-bride-to-be would have caved to
the wisdom of those who knew better.

Laura-the-mother couldn't do it. Couldn't cut it. I couldn't stretch
out feedings when I couldn't shake the feeling that Maya really did
seem to need to nurse that often. I couldn't leave her to cry, even
when nearly every voice around me said that I *must*. Mark was

ever-supportive, assuring me that I wasn't doing anything wrong. Still, though, apologies flooded constantly from my lips — to him, to my baby girl, to God, and to everyone impacted by my failure. My heart was stubbornly refusing to allow me to follow the loud and clear voices that had placed child-rearing wisdom so readily at my fingertips. So out-of-character was this rebellious streak that I hardly recognized myself anymore. Now, instead of the assurance of a plan for successfully parenting God's way, I was experiencing a dizzying crash into uncertainty and a severe crisis of self-doubt. I was going rogue, and had no idea where to turn for direction.

Two windows lit up down the block as my neighbors began to rise for the workday. Mark would soon be up as well. I should have been taking the opportunity to soak up a little more sleep while Maya dozed. Instead, I clutched her closer, studying the curve of her nose while I drowned in the utter terror I felt in imagining the future.

If I failed to heed the advice of those with the answers, what would happen to my child … my marriage … my home?

Who would be my guide?

* * *

Two women who had cried tears of joy and celebrated with their husbands just one year earlier over impending parenthood now found those initial hopes and dreams floundering. Though thrilled to be mothers and desperately in love with their daughters, Megan and Laura were each discovering that their pursuit of the "right way" in parenting had left them crippled with confusion and burdened under the weight of fear.

Chapter Two

As We Confess Our Fears

Few things in life are more terrifying than that first year of parenting, particularly the earliest weeks and months. Some of us, by nature, will seek perfection, but many just want to survive. And unfortunately for most of us, our lives are lived in carefully constructed independence, detached from authentic community, where we could learn what real life, day-to-day parenting of a new baby looks like from close family members and friends.

Without that flesh and blood reality to fill in the blanks left by our question marks, we turn to the parenting manuals, seeking the advice of the experts. We languish away reading Internet message boards, desperate for someone to just tell us how to do this new parent thing!

In fact, it was within the world of online message boards that Megan and Laura's friendship finds its roots. In the discussion forums of a major parenting website, both of us happened upon the birth club for January 2005 babies. A couple of hundred mothers-to-be united by approximate due dates gathered in that little corner of the world wide web, and collectively we cobbled together a community of conversation, helping each other figure out answers to questions like:

How do I know if these contractions are Braxton Hicks or the real thing?

Is this discharge normal?

Why am I losing my hair?

Help! Daycare questions!

I hate my pediatrician. What do I do?

Am I making enough milk?

Why won't my baby ever sleep?

Spend a few minutes skimming Facebook, reading blogs, or visiting parenting forums, and you'll discover that impending motherhood tends to trigger fear in even the most confident of souls. The anxieties and concerns we see most frequently addressed are:

Fear of chaos. For Laura, as someone who enjoys a predictable schedule, I felt almost nauseous at the gentle teasing comments that accompanied nearly every congratulatory hug as people found out we were expecting. "Better sleep now, because you never will again!" "After kids come, you and your husband will hardly remember each other's names." "Get ready to kiss your free time good-bye!" "Just wait until you're trying to make dinner with a screaming baby on your hip." It felt to me as if the underlying message from everyone seemed to be *"I'm so excited for you! You've just totally ruined your life!"*

Few things brought me as much comfort as my pre-baby daily routine: a quiet drive home from work, lingering over dinner with Mark, and settling in for a leisurely evening. Movie dates and road trips with friends were highlights of our weekends. I knew, obviously, that having a baby would bring changes to our lives. But constant warnings about the drastic and negative impacts of our impending parenthood were enough to cause me sleepless nights long before giving birth.

We all like our routines, our habits and our well-worn ways of doing things. What will a new baby do to all the patterns of life we've come to know and love?

Fear of judgment from others. For Megan, I can remember when I was pregnant with Dacey that I loved to watch a show on TLC called "Bringing Home Baby." I would sit, jaw agape and eyes wide in utter fascination, watching these poor couples stumble through the first few days of life at home with a newborn. Each cry from baby sent the parents into a tizzy. Hungry? Wet? What to do? *What to do?*

I can remember rolling my eyes a little bit as they muddled through their confusion. This was exactly the trouble my trusty parenting manual had warned me to avoid! By the end of each episode, I would turn to its pages once again to immerse myself in the promises that life with a new baby didn't have to look like the waking nightmare I saw on the television screen.

In our pre-parenting lives, few of us choose to extend grace to the mothers and fathers around us. It's so very easy to raise the perfect imaginary child, and so very hard to raise actual children. Because we have lacked grace for other parents, we assume that no one will extend grace to us.

Fear of failure. As we've talked with hundreds of other parents in the years we've spent developing this book, this is the one issue that surfaces time and time again. Whether it's being unable to breastfeed as long as planned or realizing your baby is the polar opposite of independent or being confronted in the doctor's office when the milestones chart indicates your baby is lagging behind. Just under the surface of every unexpected turn on the parenting path is the gripping fear that we are failing these little ones who are so desperately dependent on us to do this the right way.

The stakes in parenting are high. Unlike other areas of life in which we can walk away if things don't work out, in parenting *this is it*. You are the only parents your child gets and it is up to you not to mess it up. That is an incredible amount of pressure, and it weighs heavily on parents-to-be. Added to this is the fear of failing our spouses, our marriages, and our circle of friends by not sticking to the established norms for how things are done to build and maintain happy homes.

All of these worries boil down to one central concern: Fear of the unknown. If we could just *know for sure* what was headed our way in parenthood and *know for certain* what the answers were to any potential problems, we would feel so much more prepared for the journey.

Fortunately, there is help at the ready. Because our culture tends to avoid sharing life together in the intimacy that provides real-life responses to these universal fears, there are bookshelves full of advice from the experts. The authors of these manuals are quite certain they have found *the* answer to all of your baby-raising needs, with some even going so far as to suggest that the approach they take is God's way to parent an infant. Many families implement these methods with great success and support the books and authors with their enthusiastic recommendations. Thus, these resources surge to staggering popularity, studied eagerly by expectant mothers and sleep-deprived new parents desperate to get a handle on the answers.

There is something to be said for the comfort the mainstream parenting paradigm offers. In the face of fear, the natural response is to seek out a way to *avoid* what is causing us anxiety or to *enact* a plan that will help us overcome the fear. And so we have instructions that ease our minds with parameters like these:

Parents can and should be in control of every aspect of baby's day from birth:

> *"Whether you have one baby, twins, or a set of triplets, you need to begin establishing your routine from day one."*[1]

> *"You should start your routine, ideally, from the day you bring your little bundle home from the hospital."* [2]

Baby's arrival should bring as little interruption to the family as possible:

> *"Your baby is part of your life, not the other way around. If we allow the baby to set the pace, eating and sleeping whenever he likes, within six weeks, your household will be in chaos."*[3]

Independence should be fostered from the earliest weeks:

> *"How do you get babies to sleep twelve hours by twelve weeks old? I believe that babies would do this on their own if parents just left them alone and encouraged their babies' natural tendencies."*[4]

---

1   Gary Ezzo, *On Becoming Babywise* (Sisters, OR: Multnomah Books, 1995) 97

2   Tracy Hogg and Melinda Blau, *The Baby Whisperer Solves All Your Problems* (New York: Atria Books, 2005) 9

3   Tracy Hogg and Melinda Blau, *Secrets of the Baby Whisperer: How to Calm, Connect, and Communicate with your Baby* (New York: Ballantine Books, 2002) 45

4   Suzy Giordano and Lisa Abidin, *The Baby Sleep Solution* (New York: Perigee Books, 2006) 14

The list goes on, and we hold in our hands all of the rules, procedures, and philosophical Musts, Nevers, and Always that we could possibly need. When you are peering into the great unknown of life with a baby, it can be quite comforting to know that *someone will tell you what to do.*

We crave a solution, and we are given one. The one that should work – it appears – in every home. One-size-fits-all answers guarantee restful nights, protected marriages, harmonious homes, and well-disciplined children. God is honored, success is achieved, and everyone lives happily ever after. What a comforting antidote to that new-mother anxiety! Answers chase the fear away. Charts and schedules color in the unknown. A sturdy plan becomes a lifeline. Now we can do this. Now we can shake the fear.

Only, what if that doesn't happen? What if, for some of us, the voices with the answers begin to sound further and further out of tune with our instincts about what is right for our families? What if we try with everything in us to do this parenting thing the "right way," but everything goes wrong and feels wrong? What if the realization that our days and nights and our babies' behaviors look nothing like the ones we are reading about only sends us careening into deeper, darker tunnels of confusion—and the fears just intensify?

For Laura, I was completely rattled by the discovery that the certainty I once clung to in the pages of the books—the plans that once calmed my anxieties—now caused me nothing but stress. Finally, someone was telling me what to do, and I just couldn't do it. I found myself almost wishing for the days when I only *worried* that I might not succeed as a mother, as I was now nearly certain that those concerns had indeed come to pass. What had begun as mere flutters of nerves during pregnancy had turned into full-fledged panic as heavier fears now threatened to suffocate me.

What is wrong?

As we recounted in Chapter One, both of us struggled mightily with the idea that there just had to be something amiss if we were not finding success with the advice we so deeply desired to follow. Our fears of potential failure took a darker turn into fears that *we were most definitely failing*. We worried that we were not strong enough as mothers. That we were lacking in some fundamental emotional point of clarity or spiritual virtue necessary to parent our babies correctly. We agonized over the idea that our instincts were off and our hearts were being led astray by deceptive feelings.

I am the problem.

Worse, maybe there was something wrong with our daughters. Under the impression that everyone else's babies had received the memo about their parents' expectations, we each wrestled with the fear that the little girls we had prayed for and planned for with our husbands had been born with behavioral abnormalities. That they were not exhibiting appropriate sleep or feeding patterns. That they were already showing signs of disobedience or lack of discipline. We stared at our daughters, hearts sinking in despair.

My baby is the problem.

One-size-fits-all parenting advice provides peaceful affirmation for those parents whose own personalities and babies' temperaments happen to fit the prescribed mold. In those for whom the neatly-packaged advice does not resonate at a heart level, however, it can stir up not only massive amounts of fear, but heavy guilt and shame as well. For a new mother, the perception that either she or her baby is failing in some way is an incredibly difficult burden to shoulder amidst the already exhausting day-to-day life with a newborn.

What will people say?

For Megan, it was the issue of nighttime sleep that lured me into outright dishonesty. My best friend from high school gave birth to her first baby just five days after Dacey was born. We both rallied around the message of one particularly popular parenting book, and in our earliest weeks at our new mothering gig, we spent hours on the phone together, both cheerleading and coaching one another to live up to the program prescribed in the pages.

As the months went by, it became clear that her baby was adapting quite well to the approach, but Dacey and I were failing miserably. Though she had been one of my closest friends for well over a decade at that point and knew more than a few secrets that I never would have confided to anyone else, I was suddenly terrified at the thought of her knowing I was sinking. So in our phone calls, I swallowed hard, plastered on a smile, and lied. I would have happily poured out my heart to an impartial stranger at that point about how I spent most of my days a bleary, blubbering mess, but I just couldn't fathom the thought of telling my best friend the truth.

The truth for many mothers is that when the mainstream advice does not work or feel right for our families, we experience tremendous anxiety over how our parenting choices will be viewed by those around us. The original shudders of resolve against raising children that turn out like the fictional examples from the "how not to parent" sections of the baby books eventually become sighs of resignation. Another night of rocking to the baby to sleep seems to carry the promise of a future in which this baby will grow into an entitled monster, eliciting *tsk-tsks* from friends and observers. *If only that child's parents would have tried a little harder.*

For the in-crowd of mothers who've happily raised their babies by the book, there is safety in numbers. Those who step outside of those bounds often feel they must avoid conversations, dread questions, and even lie outright about their babies' habits in order to escape the judgment — whether real or perceived — from well-meaning friends or strangers in the grocery store check-out line. No matter how aware we are that we shouldn't concern ourselves with the expectations of others, the fact is that we often *do* care. We care a lot. And in those times when we field critical comments or corrective suggestions, we can't help but wonder if they're right.

What does God think?

Since a handful of parenting manuals have found their wildest popularity in Christian circles, the assumption, or even outright claim, that they contain the methods which reflect God's way to care for an infant builds an even greater pressure for parents who long to please Him in their child-rearing efforts. The fear of failing these instructions climbs to painful intensity when we also carry the perception that we are failing God.

One-size-fits-all parenting advice already makes sweeping assumptions about the effectiveness and appropriateness of the methods for every child of every parent in every home. When such advice is penned or interpreted through a Christian perspective, it can create some of the strongest fear of all for those parents who do not, in fact, fit. Suddenly, everything is at risk: our children, our marriages, our reputations, and even our relationships with God. The implications of these risks can be truly terrifying.

The Burden of Fear

Fear may have driven us to parenting books to begin with, but a deeper, more desperate fear follows when our reality doesn't match up with the books' philosophies. When the instructions do not line up for us, the answers we once eagerly sought no longer provide comfort and guidance. Instead, what leaps off the page to our tired eyes are all of the warnings of what will happen if we don't take to heart the advice of the author: undisciplined children prone to selfishness and tantrums, wrecked marriages devoid of sex and connection, and far-reaching instability in every area of a family's life.

Some parenting manuals seem to actually rely on fear to convince the reader that their way is best. Fear can be a strong motivator, but it's an exhausting burden to carry along the path. The further we turned from the recommended advice, the more we felt these warnings turn to threats of what was surely to come. Rather than feeling empowered to step off the beaten path to explore a new approach that might be better suited to our families, we found ourselves paralyzed, listening to the voices which seemed to play on an endless loop in our minds, perpetually indicting us of all of our shortcomings.

What we desperately needed was someone who would tell us that what we thought were our shortcomings weren't really shortcomings at all, but rather symptoms that fear-sickness had overtaken our hearts and minds. In those moments of gripping self-doubt, we needed someone to give us permission to admit that the advice of the books wasn't working, and we needed to know that we could dare to turn loose of the tools that weren't made for us.

In the New Testament, the Apostle John wrote to the early church that "There is no fear in love. But perfect love drives out fear ..." (1 John 4:18, ESV). If this is true, why then were we so fearful? And who could offer enough love to help us overcome our fears? As it turns out, there was one word that could have filled the void for us, one word that would have changed *everything* if only we had been listening to the voice of the only One who can truly offer it: **freedom.**

Chapter Three

As We Pursue Another Way

I sought the LORD, and He answered me; He delivered me from all my fears. (Psalm 34:4, NIV)

Fear is where both Laura and Megan once dwelled. As we held our first babies, we each carried the weight of failed expectations, intense confusion, and total lack of direction. We've told you how parenting manuals caused so much distress for us when we were new mothers. So why would *we*, of all people, want to add one more book to a shelf already over-crowded with words of advice and instruction? What you'll read in the chapters to come is quite different from what you'll find in other books about baby's first year. What we are so passionate about sharing with new parents and parents-to-be is a message that we desperately wish would have been shared with us when we were new to motherhood:

There is another way. **There is an approach to parenting that looks fear in the face and boldly speaks an answer:** *Freedom.* **Freedom from required formulas, unrealistic expectations of our children and ourselves, and the belief that we must force our babies to fit into a mold that may not have been designed for them.**

Scripture speaks with awe-inspiring confidence about the freedom we have through faith in Christ. (Galatians 5:1) While we know that the greatest freedom we find in Him is the one that releases us from the wages of sin and death (Romans 6:23), we also know that His deliverance from fear and promise of presence and power extend to every calling in our lives — including the journey of parenting. As we seek the Lord, we can find the freedom to shrug off plans and advice that are just not working and follow His lead instead. To call upon His wisdom, power, and example with confidence, and to accept His grace when we fall short.

An Invitation to a New Pursuit

Within these pages is the radical idea that God has a unique plan for each family — one that recognizes the individuality of both the parents and the child. It suggests that there is no one-size-fits-all plan. We've both read and tried to follow the advice of several of the most popular parenting books available today. And what we have come to advocate and embrace instead is the idea that God's way when it comes to caring for an infant is perfectly individual to every household. The right way for each mother and father to approach parenting is to seek His direction and guidance. Engaging this approach requires listening intently to the Spirit's leading and then following that direction.

Within God's overall plans and purposes for humanity, He knows with perfection what is best for each of us. He extends to us the freedom to stop striving in vain to make our own plans work and to confidently follow the leading of His Spirit instead.

This idea of beginning without a clear plan can be unnerving. We want consistent guidelines and cold hard facts. We want outlines and directions that are easy to read and follow. But Spirit-led parenting doesn't work like that. And the reason for this is yet another radical idea: the first year should be less about training our babies and more about God developing us as parents and human beings. If we let Him, God can use that first intense year of baby's life to *train us* how to live a life that is fully surrendered to Him. To cultivate in us a trust that follows His lead, seeks Him first, and understands His grace.

As we will share throughout this book, parenting under the direction of the Holy Spirit is not easy. It can and likely will squeeze every last drop of *self* out of us. If we yield to it, though, there is such potential for spiritual growth and for learning—in the most hands-on, real-life way possible—what it truly means to be a servant leader. *It can be a year of transformation from which we emerge with a refined and sharpened perspective, equipped to experience other people, other relationships, and other situations through the eyes of a servant. It can be a year of discovering new and life-changing joy and a release from the captivity of guilt and shame.*

As you step into parenthood, whether it be for the first time or the last, we want to invite you to pursue the freedom that seeks God's direction above all else as you care for your baby, and that allows *Him* to parent *you* into profound growth as well.

Freedom to Parent as He Leads

"Now the Lord is the Spirit; and where the Spirit of the Lord is, there is freedom". (2 Corinthians 3:17 NIV)

The philosophy we offer is not a method we've developed and perfected *(oh, how far we are from having perfected it!)*, but rather a mindset that we seek, with God's help, to live out as parents. We feel a clear call to care for our children with our hearts and minds focused on the heart of God. We feel led to consistently, compassionately, and creatively meet their needs, under the direction of His Spirit, as they arise. If it sounds like a simple concept—it *is*. If it sounds like an easy one—*it's not*.

Spirit-led parenting is not a one-size-fits-all approach. It has no "rules" and doesn't rely on the wisdom of others. It requires only that you listen to your child, to your intuition, and most importantly, to the Lord's leading to determine the best way to respond to each unique situation. While some families may find that the approach they are led to may appear quite similar to the ones found in the popular school of thought, others will discover that God leads them to methods which split off the mainstream path.

Just as God created each of us as unique individuals, we come into this world with different personalities and different sets of needs. Some babies are born good sleepers (we all wish for one of those!), while others may not sleep through the night for a year or even longer. Some are naturally content and will happily entertain themselves for long periods of time, while others are unhappy unless they're being held, cuddled, and carried. This is where the "not easy" part comes in.

This philosophy of child rearing requires a shift away from the mindset of parenting with the goal of convenience. It doesn't expect that an infant should be trained to sleep eight-hour stretches, or that a young baby should adapt to a schedule and fit easily into an established routine. It means letting go of our ideas of what we think our babies *should* need, and when.

Letting go of control in any area of life is difficult and prying ourselves from the grip of those messages insisting that we maintain control in our parenting, *or else* (Your marriage!   Your child's future!   The harmony in your home!), takes far more effort. The relative unknown of surrendering to God's lead versus the allure of neatly-ordered plans for success creates a stressful dilemma as we question whether He will really come through and wonder if we will really hear Him. Can we confidently allow ourselves to trust? Let's explore this further.

Freedom to call upon the Father, Son, and Spirit

What is our first instinct when we hit a parenting roadblock? Where do we turn in that moment of panic? There is certainly a purpose and place for resources offering instruction to new parents. Many first-time mothers — including us — have been helped tremendously by pieces of advice from relatives and friends, and absorbed important information about signs of illness, tips for bath time, etc. from books and websites.

Overall, though, with so many outspoken answers and bits of contradicting advice at our fingertips, we can become overwhelmed and quickly forget that the one true expert on our babies' unique needs — our Creator God — is on call at all times for us as Believers. Within the three persons of the trinity, we have an unrivaled source of direction and truth to call upon as we step into parenting.

Throughout Scripture, God establishes Himself first and foremost in relationship with us as our Father God. He is not a distant God, nor is He detached from the children He lovingly created. He is a parent who in chapter after chapter, story after story, beckons and encourages His children to become deeply, inseparably attached to Him (Isaiah 66:13a, Isaiah 49:16). But God also offers to lead us into the experience of parenting. Isaiah 40:11 says:

*"He tends his flock like a shepherd: He gathers the lambs in his arms and carries them close to his heart; **he gently leads those that have young**" (NIV, emphasis ours).*

God's offer to us as we raise our babies and children is an offer of gentle leadership. Who better than the Creator to advise us on how to care for these precious children He painstakingly and lovingly created?

It is our belief that each and every parent can call upon our Father God for that which can never be described or prescribed in any parenting instruction manual: **wisdom**. This is a wisdom that comes not from a culture concerned chiefly with convenience, from parenting "experts" who offer predetermined solutions, or from the well-meaning advice of family and friends who are confident that what worked for them must work for everyone else. This wisdom comes straight from the heart of God and is unique to each mother, father, child, family, and season of life. What's more, we know from James 1:5 that God is gracious and *generous* in giving us wisdom if we will but ask.

Not only can we be secure in the guidance we will receive under the leadership of our Father God, we can also draw close to and learn from God the Son as we seek to love the way He loves and serve the way He serves. In chapter 22 of the Gospel of Luke, Christ reminds His disciples that He was among them as *one who serves*. Indeed, every aspect of the life of Christ was grounded in servanthood. His first priority was always that of serving God. He demonstrated His vast and unconditional love for others by reaching out through service. If our lives are to be modeled after the way Christ lived in His time here on earth, then we are called to servanthood.

The love Christ showed for mankind is inextricably intertwined with selflessness and sacrifice. This is not a popular idea in a culture that places supreme importance on making sure your own needs are being met. But Christ admonished His followers that, "If anyone would come after me, he must deny himself and take up his cross daily and follow me" (Luke 9:23, NIV). He makes it clear from the beginning that to follow Him is to be willing to forgo our own needs and desires on a daily basis.

Later, the Apostle Paul would write,

"Have this attitude in yourselves which was also in Christ Jesus, who, although He existed in the form of God, did not regard equality with God a thing to be grasped, but emptied Himself, taking the form of a bond-servant, and being made in the likeness of men" (Phil 2: 5-7, NAS).

When the intangible God chose to make Himself tangible to the world, He chose the form of a servant. Think on that for a moment. He could have come in any incarnation that pleased the Father, and the incarnation that He knew would prove to be most powerful, most influential, and most extraordinary was that of *servant*. Surely, that must speak volumes to us as believers as to how we are to approach each relationship with each person (no matter how small) the Lord places in our lives.

Fortunately, we do not have to rely on our own strength, power and discipline to love through servanthood. We have indwelling within us the very Spirit of the Living God. He's there in the trenches with us — encouraging us when we need it, cautioning us when necessary, and compelling us to be ever-prayerful and wise in the attitudes and actions we choose within parenthood.

In fact, when Jesus told His followers that the Father would send the Spirit to us, He referred to the Spirit as the Counselor: "All this I have spoken while still with you. But the Counselor, the Holy Spirit whom the Father will send in my name, will teach you all things and will remind you of everything I have said to you." (John 14:26, NIV) The Spirit that dwells within us has the power to counsel, console, inspire, remind us of what we have forgotten, and teach us that which we haven't known. As believers, we have a twenty-four hour, seven day a week on-call parenting expert on whom we can call in the person of the Holy Spirit within us.

Consider the words the Apostle Paul prayed for the people of the church at Ephesus: "that you may know . . . his incomparably great power for us who believe. That power is like the working of his mighty strength, which he exerted in Christ when he raised him from the dead and seated him at his right hand in the heavenly realms." (Eph. 1:18-20, NIV) Take a minute to take that in. Because of the resurrection life of Christ within us, we are able to call on a supernatural strength that was mighty enough to raise Christ from the dead! Through the power of the Holy Spirit of God, we have every resource we could possibly need to live out this otherwise-impossible call to serve those around us with love.

With the wisdom and gentle leadership of God the Father, the perfect example of servanthood in God the Son, and the incomparable power of God the Spirit available to us as we parent, there is no reason to lack confidence in the direction we are sure to receive as we call on the Lord to guide us.

Freedom to extend grace

While fear rallies in us a hyper-vigilance against any deviance from our plans or expectations, freedom allows us to respond to unexpected parenting struggles with grace. If we pursue the freedom to follow God's lead — whatever it may look like — we find our hearts more open to discovering the beauty and grace in a difficult moment.

For Megan, it was church nursery drama with Dacey that forced the issue. Sunday after Sunday, I tried to drop her off in the baby nursery at church. Other mothers handed over diaper bags and cooing babies to the smiling nursery workers, but to Dacey, I may as well have been handing her over to scary clowns staffing a terrifying fun house. She cried, she reached, she wailed. When other mothers patted my back and offered me comfort, I would start crying myself. Not only did my heart hurt to hear my baby melting down that way, it also seemed to further confirm that I was doing something wrong. If only I were as good as those other mothers at helping their babies to be independent! My every fear about raising a clingy, overly-dependent baby was coming to life.

Finally, one Sunday morning, I was too tired to engage the battle in the nursery hallway, so I just carried her straight into the sanctuary with me. I whispered in her little ear, telling her that was an organ that was making that music and that I used to sing that hymn standing next to my mama in church. Soon, she was fast asleep in my arms. I can't remember a bit of the sermon from that Sunday morning, but I do remember the way the Spirit moved me to extend grace to her (and to the nursery workers!) by meeting her in the moment of her need.

A tremendous weight is lifted when we allow ourselves to respond with grace. Grace for our children when seasons of teething or separation anxiety make for fussy nights and clingy days. Grace for our spouses when exhaustion clouds communication and everyone is just a little bit more on edge. Grace for friends who parent differently, when the path God sets before them takes some different turns than ours.

And then there is the most difficult of all: grace for ourselves. As difficult as it can be to extend grace to others in the midst of frustration or disappointment, it can seem downright impossible to dig out from beneath the heaps of ideals and assumptions that we pile upon ourselves. You would be hard-pressed to find a parent who hasn't had at least a few moments where they've felt absolutely certain that they are messing up their children for life within their first year. This is why we want to address one more incredibly important element of pursuing freedom in parenting.

Freedom to Fail

Is there any area of life where we more frantically chase perfection than in parenthood? Whether it comes from a desire to make up for our own childhood disappointments (*Surely I can give my children the parent I always wanted*), that all-too-common tendency to compare ourselves with the flawless facades we see in encounters with other parents (*I bet she never raises her voice*), or just the strict mindset of a classic overachiever (*I will be the best at this if it kills me*), we can easily become our own worst critics.

For Laura, there was one particular afternoon when I was struggling in vain to get Maya down for a nap, and my frustration reached its boiling point. As she stirred in her crib and began to cry yet again, I stomped out of her room, slammed the door so hard the house shook, and threw a tantrum right there in the hallway. It was not pretty, and I may or may not have punched a wall.

Afterward, as I took a deep breath and went in to scoop up my whimpering daughter, I felt deep shame. My ability to keep an even-keeled temper had been a source of pride up until that point, and losing it in that way felt like such an ugly failure. Maya cooed and snuggled into my arms contentedly, and I knew that as I whispered my repentance to God, I was forgiven in that very instant. But forgiving myself took far longer.

No matter how hard we try, no matter how firm our resolve to be the perfect parent, we will fail. Again and again. We will raise voices in frustration, act selfishly, snap at our spouses, miss appointments, or choose self-pity over prayer. We will more than likely break at least a few of the self-imposed rules on our pre-parenthood lists. When the inevitable happens and we fail, will there be grace for *us*?

Scripture tells us with certainty that there is no condemnation for those who know Christ as Savior (Romans 8:1) and that our Father God removes the weight of sin from us, tossing our transgressions "as far as the east is from the west" (Psalm 103:12, NIV). As we stumble in our weakness and come to Him seeking forgiveness, His grace is lavish and unending and nothing can separate us from His love. (Romans 8:38-39).

Our little ones are gracious with us as well. Those failings and foibles that we wallow in and carry as baggage do not for one single second diminish the fact that our babies see us as the most important and amazing people on the face of the earth. And as they grow into childhood, we give them an incredibly valuable gift when we allow them to see us fail. The example of a "perfect" parent is not nearly as formative as the one of a parent who both lives the lesson that we all fall short and humbly models the power of forgiveness.

Ultimately, what stands most boldly in the way of the grace intended for us is our own refusal to accept it. Could we find the courage to lay down the expectations we set for ourselves and count what we deem to be failures as opportunities for the Lord's refinement? Could we begin to view parenting our children as not so much about what we can do or accomplish, but what He can do in us and through us if we will surrender ourselves?

The Cost of Freedom

Megan recalls a night spent almost entirely in the rocking chair, sitting up with her daughter who was fighting a cold. At one point during the long, dark hours, she felt God speak clearly to her that there is a cost incurred in parenting under the leading of the Spirit. There is a price that comes with freedom. While we will show in the chapters to come that what we originally feared losing—the health of our marriages, our parental authority, and our children's emotional and spiritual well-being—are not at risk in following this philosophy, there is a precious cost incurred. The paradox of true freedom in Christ is that we must surrender our wills.

It's about dying to self.

So much of what is spoken to parents (in secular and Christian material) is about maintaining and reclaiming yourself after you have a child, but there are few suggestions that one worthy response to God entrusting you with this little one is dying to your devotion to yourself. And since God Himself directs us to do so, we aren't turning ourselves over to our babies or to other people as much as we are turning ourselves over to the Lord, who (among other things) leads and commands us to be servants of others.

We in the Western Church often give great lip service to the idea of servanthood. We understand that if we are to model our lives after the life of Christ, then we must choose the path of service. The New Testament letters are filled with admonitions to consider others more important than ourselves and to serve one another wholeheartedly and in love. And so we agree to serve God by serving others, right up to the point where service encroaches on our comfort. When confronted with the cost of sustained servanthood ... well, this is when we start to squirm.

Spirit-led living, in general, is a difficult way of living to embrace, because in its true form it expects nothing in return. Ideally, in a marriage for instance, both people within a relationship are living out a mindset of service *to each other* on a regular basis. But reciprocation is not the motivation through which we are to give of ourselves. We must give, must serve simply because our Lord asks us to do so. And we are most definitely not taught through Scripture to take our convenience into account in these matters.

If we were to look at our spouse, or at a neighbor that God has placed in our lives who has needs to be met, and say, "I'm sorry, what you need from me isn't convenient at this time. You'll have to learn to require those things at an appropriate time," we would surely consider that attitude to be one from which we need to repent. Why would we see our children, the most precious gifts that God has placed in our care, any differently? Perhaps parenting an infant is one of the purest examples of living out the gospel because it is truly a *give, give, give* relationship. It is a constant opportunity to allow God to refine us by laying down our own desires to care for the needs of another.

Following the leadership of Christ and choosing a Spirit-led approach to parenting will cost you. It will cost you the luxury of uninterrupted sleep at night. It will cost you the security that is found in allowing the clock to put order to your day. It will cost you some of your "me time." It may even cost you some friendships with people in your faith community who vehemently disagree with this approach.

But what if, as that first year of babyhood winds down and a toddler stands where your baby once lay, what if you looked in the mirror and realized that the one who has grown by leaps and bounds in the past year is *you*? What if you could see that in most every situation you encounter, your first response is no longer selfish retreat, but rather selfless embrace?

Would it make you smile with humble gratitude to recognize that in each moment you chose to approach your baby with a heart filled by the Spirit, you were able to more closely relate to and identify with your Lord Jesus Christ than you ever had before? If you found, for perhaps the first time, that you were truly free in Him?

Would it be worth the cost?

The answer to this question is the very reason that we have written this book. What we know now is the result of deep, often painful, brilliantly beautiful work that God did in our lives as we each journeyed through the first year of motherhood. In the next several chapters, we will revisit moments of frustration, heartache, and confusion. And we will tell how God spoke to us in areas of parenting that began as points of anxiety and ended much differently. We will tell you how he took us from fear to freedom.

"If the Son sets you free, you will be free indeed." (John 8:36, NIV)

Section Two

Few among us would choose fear to be the marker of our earliest experiences in parenting. Most of us genuinely desire the life-giving offer of freedom.

What does that look like lived out?

How does freedom answer these questions:

What if I hate breastfeeding?

What if my six month old isn't sleeping through the night?

What if, after the baby arrives, my marriage falls apart?

What if we never have sex again?

What if we cannot live on a schedule?

Those questions (and so many more) are the ones we found ourselves asking once we diverged from the path of the mainstream and dared to forge ahead on the road to freedom. In the pages to come, you'll read more of our story and the stories of others, painting for you a picture of what the Spirit-led parenting path looked like in our lives. What you won't find here are a strict set of instructions, nor will there be any formulas for parenting success.

Instead, we want you to see our own lived-out version of Psalm 107:

"They were hungry and thirsty, and their lives ebbed away. Then they cried out to the LORD in their trouble, and He delivered them from their

distress. He led them by a straight way ... for he satisfies the thirsty and fills the hungry with good things." (verses 5-9, NIV)

We stand before you not as gate-keepers to the land of answers, but rather as lamp-holders along a path that can be lonely and even scary. We merely wish to help light the way because we know the reward at the end is worth the risk.

Chapter Four

As We Feed Them

Nourishing the newborn, as natural and basic as it may seem from afar, can be one of the most stressful aspects of a new mother's life. From the controversial first question of breast vs. bottle and varied obstacles many women face in the beginning, to the confusing debates over frequency charts and feeding philosophies, it is easy to become quickly overwhelmed!

In the next few pages, we will take time to discuss common concerns and perceptions, address with honesty the hard stuff that breastfeeding mothers can encounter (things your grandma who nursed nine babies with ease may not have told you!), offer some tips for making it through the rough spots, and speak peace and encouragement to mothers who have struggled – or may struggle – with the decision to use formula. Most of all, we want to once again encourage every new parent or parent-to-be to cover this important aspect of their baby's life in prayer and seek the Lord's leading as the primary source of wisdom.

-Laura's Story-

Just five days into the breastfeeding experience, I was ready to quit. For good.

It was midnight, and two out of the three members of our family were in tears. It had started with Maya, after Mark and I accidentally slept through the last recurrence of the every-two-hours alarm we had been instructed to set. Maya was having trouble latching to my breast for her feedings, and the hungrier she became, the more her desperation complicated the process. It seemed the only way to achieve any sort of feeding success was to catch her in a sleepy, not-yet-starving state of relative calm. Hence, the two-hour wake-up calls. This time, though, she had woken up screaming, and our attempts to latch her on were frustratingly futile.

Tears ran down my face as we huddled together in the darkened living room. Maya's tiny voice grew hoarse from her shuddering cries as Mark scooped her up once again from my arms to walk the floors. As he swayed and whispered to her, I stared at the ceiling.

"I need to stop this. It's not working. I'm really done." My words tumbled out wild and uneven. "They told me this would be easier than using formula. **Easier**. Those nurses told me that. They lied to me, all of them, and I think…You work at the hospital, so tell someone to fire them. Because they shouldn't lie to their patients. It's unethical. Do nurses take an oath? They should take an oath and it should be to tell the truth. Because I am not stupid. I know that there is no way that this madness is easier than walking to the kitchen, dumping some formula into a bottle, mixing it with a little water, and *sticking it in her mouth!*"

Graciously choosing to overlook the fact that his wife had just hopped the train to Crazytown, Mark sat down next to me on the couch, placing Maya in my arms for another try. He spoke carefully.

"Honey, you really wanted to give it six weeks before you made any decisions. Let's try this again, call the lactation consultant in the morning, and see if we can push through to six weeks. If you still want to quit at that point, you'll feel better about it."

Six weeks? That landmark might as well have been six years away.

I had always known I would give breastfeeding a try. It wasn't a deep desire of my heart or anything; it just seemed practical. Before Maya was born, someone suggested that I attend the breastfeeding information class that our local hospital offers to expectant mothers, so I decided to check it out. Arriving home that evening, my arms were loaded with pamphlets and literature. "Breastfeeding is amazing!" I chirped to Mark. In newfound awe of the way God designed a mother's body to nourish her baby, I was suddenly eager and excited about this part of parenting. And while I vaguely remembered the lactation consultant saying something in class about the first six weeks being difficult for many new moms, I didn't think for a minute that I would be one of them.

Reality arrived with a crash immediately after Maya's birth. The joy and excitement of introducing our baby to the world was marred by the dread with which I faced each laborious attempt to feed her. Nurses sat beside me for hours, rotating at their shift-changes, trying to help Maya latch, stay latched, and eat. One morning, just as the sun rose, a lactation consultant named Janet arrived with salvation in the form of a contact nipple shield, a flexible piece of soft plastic that fits to the breast and makes feeding easier for babies with latch issues. While cumbersome and messy, the shield was finally a way that we could accomplish a full-feeding. Janet told me that our goal would be to wean Maya from the shield within a week, and I was hopeful.

A week went by, and Maya still could not nurse without the shield. I was told to pump before each feeding to stimulate letdown, and afterward to maintain milk supply. Maya often took forty-five minutes to eat, with the next feeding beginning just an hour-and-a-half later. It was exhausting beyond words. I did make it through six weeks, though, and felt as though I was supposed to keep going. Feedings hadn't become easy, by any means, but I no longer dreaded them.

At three months in, we were still hanging on. By this point, breastfeeding had become a familiar, if still complicated, routine. New frustrations were mounting, however. With Maya still unable to latch on her own I found myself unable to nurse her in public, or even in roomfuls of friends. There was too much equipment involved to feel comfortable in those situations. Several of our friends had also recently welcomed new babies and I deeply envied the mothers who could simply, mid-conversation, toss a blanket across their shoulder for a quick feeding.

Even more frustrating was the barrage of conflicting advice coming my way on the issue of feeding frequency. Many babies settle into an every-three-or four-hour nursing schedule on their own. Maya didn't. Lactation consultants assured me that it wasn't a problem to nurse her on demand and that it was impossible to over-feed a breastfed baby. But other people in my life disagreed. As I would leave the room for yet another nursing session, I would receive cautions against letting Maya use me "as a pacifier." I also remembered what that book had said about frequent feedings teaching bad habits.

While we seemed to be muddling through some of our initial hurdles, the growing confusion and anxiety continued to cast a dark shadow over my breastfeeding experience. There were too many voices, and I didn't trust myself to sort them out. Why did this have to be so hard?

-Megan's Story-

In the months leading up to Dacey's due date, I was far, far more anxious about breastfeeding than I was about labor and delivery. My theory was that when it came to the actual birth of our first daughter, well, she was going to have to come out one way or the other, but regardless of how it all happened, there would be a team of "experts" around me to get me through the whole process.

Breastfeeding success, on the other hand, would pretty much come down to me and me alone. She sure wasn't going to know what she was doing, so I felt an enormous pressure to do all the reading and research that I possibly could to be prepared. In fact, I never made it to a childbirth class (clearly, I harbored no visions of a natural childbirth), but I was the first student to arrive at my breastfeeding class. I sat in the front row and took copious notes and even asked questions afterwards.

My mother breastfed all four children in my family, but there were four of us born in six years, and I don't have any memories of seeing her nursing a baby. The breastfeeding books and pamphlets I found had a few pictures, but mostly drawings, and all of the visuals were kind of hazy and vague. There were step-by-step instructions, sure enough, but no real nipple close-ups. I kept thinking if I could just see the real thing in action, I would feel a little more confident. That never happened.

I was scared it would be really hard. And you know what? It was.

At first.

Following our Caesarean birth, both Dacey and I had sedative drugs in our systems and this made her even more prone to sleepiness than the average newborn. Kyle's main job in the first two weeks was to be ready with cool washcloths in case she needed a little chilly wake-up to keep her up longer than five minutes per nursing session.

Far more challenging than the sleepiness was the task of getting her to latch on correctly. I was very sore following twelve hours of labor that ended in a Caesarean section, and Dacey was nearly ten pounds at birth, which made it incredibly difficult for me to get her positioned properly. I knew exactly what I was supposed to be doing to get a good latch, but I just couldn't seem to get her to cooperate.

I can remember having to call for the nurse around four that first morning. I was sobbing and blubbering, trying to explain to her through my tears that it just wasn't working. Thankfully, both of our girls were born in a very pro-breastfeeding hospital and this particular postpartum nurse calmed and helped me, and then followed up by having the lactation consultant come check on us first thing in the morning.

There are two things I feel that no breastfeeding manual could have prepared me for: 1) how surprisingly painful it can be for some (me) when your milk "comes in," and 2) how intensely painful the nipple pain can be. Now, most every resource, lactation consultant and La Leche League leader will tell you that if you have a good, correct latch, then breastfeeding should not be painful. I will say this much, I had a lactation consultant observe Dacey's latch twice and both times it was deemed satisfactory, yet I still had a lot of nipple pain. Some of us are just more sensitive than others, I suppose.

All in all, none of it looked like what I thought it would look like. In the breastfeeding guides, the mothers are all smiling down on their newborns with dreamy, ethereal looks of contentment and joy. No one is crying; no one is bleeding. No one has soaked completely through their breast pads and t-shirt at night and saturated the sheets with their own breast milk. That might scare people, I suppose.

There was a reason that I was so determined to breastfeed, and it wasn't because God masterfully and wonderfully designed a woman's body to be able to nourish her baby, and therefore I had a special responsibility to do all that I could to make breastfeeding a success. Not at all. Simply put, we were at a time in our lives when we could neither afford formula nor could we qualify for governmental aid to buy formula. I was sort of convinced that no matter what, I had to power through and just make it work.

And so, somehow, we did. After the first six weeks or so, Dacey and I both got the hang of the logistics of breastfeeding. In fact, Dacey took to it so well that she absolutely and completely refused to take a bottle of any kind. When she was still in the womb, being the sole source of her nourishment was easy; I didn't even have to think about it. My body handled everything.

But now it meant something different. It meant buying new (bigger) bras with snaps, straps and room for bulky breast pads. It meant being so ravenously hungry that I could devour three times what my husband ate in a single meal. It meant staying home more often than ever before because my over-abundant milk supply meant that with each feeding, there was milk everywhere.

My husband was incredibly supportive. He would watch me nurse Dacey with wonder on his face and encourage me with awestruck words: "This is amazing! You are making her grow with your body!"

I would smile weakly in response. "I know."

Oh, did I know. In those first few months, I felt the toll of being the sole source of sustaining another human being: constantly hungry, constantly dealing with milk everywhere, constantly being mindful of the feeding schedule. I was also constantly wondering how sustainable this breastfeeding gig would be because I felt like I was being sucked dry. *Literally.*

* * *

Clearly, our opening days of baby-feeding felt anything but instinctive and natural. As we will share later, though, there were some precious silver linings that would eventually emerge from the dark gray clouds. First, let's look at some breastfeeding basics, along with some common struggles and questions.

Breastfeeding

In reading about how each of our experiences with feeding our babies began, you would probably consider us unlikely breastfeeding advocates. We would have agreed with you wholeheartedly at first! Out of the rubble that was the beginning, however, we have each emerged as a strong supporter of breastfeeding. The motivation for our advocacy stems not from a sense that every woman must choose to breastfeed. *Not at all.* It comes, instead, from an intense desire that any woman who wants to pursue breastfeeding have all of the resources, information, and support she needs to be able to do so.

The benefits of breastfeeding are clear. From lower incidence of childhood obesity and asthma, and better brain development for baby, to lower risk of cardiovascular disease, breast and ovarian cancers, and diabetes for mother[5] most every medical professional would agree that breast milk provides the best possible nutrition for an infant in the first year of life.

Beyond the health advantages, breastfeeding is the clear winner when considering financial implications. It's free! Many women also cite the intense bonding experience of nursing their newborns,

---

5   "How Breastfeeding Benefits Mothers' Health" Scientific American April 30, 2010

and still others rave about the ease of having a ready-made food supply available for their babies at all hours—no additional supplies needed!

For some new mothers, however, the breastfeeding road is marked with not just hurdles, but heartbreak.

Challenges

As Megan noted in her story, there are common discomforts associated with the early days of breastfeeding. Just because they are common, though, does not mean they are *no big deal*. You may have heard the word "engorgement" tossed around at a doctor's visit or prenatal class. What you probably did not hear about was the day you would stand in front of your mirror in shock, staring at a body you no longer recognize and trying to fit your breasts— which have now swelled to three times their normal size and are rock hard, extremely sore, and leaking milk—into your new nursing bras, which you only bought one size bigger than your normal one, because who could have known you'd turn into a circus freak? Meanwhile, your husband stares at you with a mixture of confusion and fascination until you turn and snarl, *"Don't even think about it."*

Beyond the typical adjustments, though, many mothers and babies struggle mightily with breastfeeding. Some have trouble at the beginning, as Laura did with Maya, in achieving and maintaining a good latch. Others encounter problems with milk supply, perhaps getting the troubling news that their baby is not gaining sufficient weight. Medical conditions and complications from the birth process can also interfere with breastfeeding success.

So, while many new moms find breastfeeding to come just as easily and naturally as the women in the hospital brochures, there are those who will face an uphill climb.

I knew from the very start that I wanted to breastfeed. My mom had nursed all six of us, some for over two years. Unfortunately, I didn't know it would be so difficult. I had cracked, bleeding nipples for two months with nursing my first child, and he ate every two hours for an hour at a time. Nursing was all I did for the first few months! – Charity, Michigan

Scheduled vs. Demand Feeding Debate

As if the early challenges aren't disorienting enough, the new nursing mother is bound to encounter many strong opinions on whether to feed based on a schedule or to feed on-demand (in response to baby's hunger cues).

We have noticed, in particular, the trend in popular Christian infant-care manuals toward recommendations of scheduled feedings. While some of these books are quick to point out that a baby who is truly hungry should always be fed, they also tend to advocate one-size-fits-all frequency charts, and strongly discourage the idea of feeding on-demand. The argument seems to be that on-cue feedings can lead to bad habits, resulting in an undisciplined child with no discernible routine.

While scheduled feedings work beautifully for many families, and while we do not take an across-the-board stance on either side of this debate (Laura generally has fed her babies on cue; Megan had success feeding her firstborn by a flexible schedule, and with cue-feeding her second), we do have a few concerns with the position taken by the mainstream Christian baby books.

We find no valid basis for an assumption that babies fed on-cue are any less well-adjusted, or their homes any less harmonious, than the schedule-fed babies with whom they share the church nursery. The American Academy of Pediatrics (AAP), in fact, recommends on-cue feeding, noting that babies should be allowed to set their own feeding routines rather than adhering to a pre-determined schedule[6]. And as we've spoken with other mothers in face-to-face conversations and in discussions on our blogs, many have told us that even though they received some criticism for the decision to feed on-cue, they found great success and reward in doing so.

> *I nursed all three of my girls whenever they wanted (including all hours of the night). They're eight, six, and three now. And in my biased opinion, they're the most normal, well-adjusted, sweet little girls I've ever met. And they put themselves to sleep (in their own beds) every single night with no trouble at all. I will always cherish every single precious moment of rocking and nursing we shared. Priceless. – Marla, Ohio*

The pressure to "get the baby on a schedule" can become stressful for a new mother to the point that she can miss out on those moments of peaceful wonder while nursing her child. The authors of these books surely do not intend to create an obsession in parents over the clock (*"When did he eat last? She's crying, but she's not supposed to eat again until 3:45 ... what is wrong?"*), but take a brand-new mother desperate for parenting success, throw in some sleep-deprivation and a hormonal upheaval, and the words in these books often have that effect. Preoccupation with the charts that lay out "normal" feeding habits can leave you studying your perfectly healthy baby with concern over their frequent requests to eat. They may invoke feelings of guilt, prompting a mother to wonder what she is doing wrong, since the feeding patterns she

---

6   (AAP Media Alert – "AAP Addresses Scheduled Feedings vs. Demand Feedings" -4/20/98)

finds herself naturally gravitating toward are so far off from those spelled out in the pages of the book on her nightstand.

> *When I was pregnant, someone lent me a book and I read it and thought, "Oh, yeah, this is great! No demand-feeding." Then I actually had my baby, and he struggled with nursing, and at times was hungry every hour and a half. I found myself saying to my husband, "NO! The book says he can't eat yet!" Finally I gave up on scheduling & fed him when he acted hungry & things went much better. I would do things very differently next time. – Carrie, New York*

Advocacy of one-size-fits-all charts and schedules, particularly in resources penned from a Christian perspective, fail to take into account the glorious uniqueness in each person created by God the Father. When He knit us together in our mothers' wombs, He did so with painstaking care, forming us with fantastically individual personalities. These variances shape the way we take in nourishment, as well. Most of us could point to adults we know – perhaps even within the same family – who have vastly different eating habits from one another. While your friend from the gym might find herself frequently hungry, snacking on small meals throughout the day, her brother across town may regularly become so occupied with work that he forgets to eat lunch unless he's reminded to take a break.

Some babies are born requiring more frequent meals than others. Some are efficient eaters and some take their time. There are newborns who will doze straight through feeding time and need to be awakened to ensure that they are taking in enough milk. There are others who would never choose sleep over food, *ever!* To suggest that all babies will (or should) adapt to any one particular feeding regimen is to overlook the individual needs, innately created personalities, medical issues, and other unique situations that can affect the ideal feeding plan for each child.

In the days when I was expecting my first baby, the book that was handed to me by a dear friend was written by a nurse whose career had involved coming into homes and whipping the resident newborn into shape so that the parents could sleep through the night and only feed the baby every four hours during the day. I remember it sounded so idyllic. Later in my pregnancy, however, I read about how nighttime feedings are actually beneficial. It made so much more sense to me that the natural rhythms that develop between the individual mother and baby would have layers of value, particularly in the bigger picture, that a convenience-oriented culture might easily overlook.

I was also fortunate in that my stepmother had, in the late 60's and early 70's, nursed my younger sisters for a couple of years each in her freewheeling listening-to-my-heart style, and it didn't seem like a big deal. My younger sisters were delightful tweens when my first baby arrived so I had no fears that merely by demand-feeding I would be "ruining" my baby. – Kathy, Kentucky

For the breastfeeding mother, a scheduled approach may interfere with long-term breastfeeding success. In the earliest weeks of breastfeeding, the endocrine system is hard at work supplying milk for baby. The endocrine system also encourages the development of prolactin receptors. How would this be affected by a feeding schedule? This explanation from a Kellymom article on milk production explains the concern with scheduled feedings from birth:

The hormone prolactin must be present for milk synthesis to occur. On the walls of the lactocytes (milk-producing cells of the alveoli) are prolactin receptor sites that allow the prolactin in the blood stream to move into the lactocytes and stimulate the synthesis of breast milk components. When the alveolus is full of milk, the walls expand/stretch and alter the shape of prolactin receptors so that prolactin cannot enter via those receptor sites – thus rate of milk synthesis decreases. As milk empties from the alveolus, increasing numbers of prolactin receptors return to their normal shape and allow prolactin to pass through - thus rate of milk synthesis increases. The prolactin receptor theory suggests that frequent milk removal in the early weeks will increase the number of receptor sites. More receptor sites means that more prolactin can pass into the lactocytes and thus milk production capability would be increased.[7]

Even for the breastfeeding mother who would feel more comfortable with the scheduled approach to nursing, a more on-cue approach may be best in the earliest weeks in order to build the best possible start on long-lasting milk production capacity.

A Biblical precedent can't be implied when there is none to be found. God's Word is completely silent on how often, and on what basis, a mother should feed her baby. When a Christian parenting manual lauds one feeding philosophy and warns against another, it can easily be interpreted as an instruction on the "right" way for a follower of Christ to approach their baby's eating habits, creating a wrenching tension for new parents who may be feeling led in a

---

7   Kelly Bonyata, "How does milk production work?" [Internet- WWW, URL] http://www.kellymom.com/bf/supply/milkproduction.html, 20 May 2001.

different direction, but who desperately want to honor God with their parenting choices.

Simply put, there isn't one clear-cut, across-the-board "right" choice between scheduled and demand feeding methods. This is ultimately a decision to bring before God in prayer, allowing His Spirit to bring wisdom and clarity for your individual situation and uniquely-created child.

Practical Advice for the Breastfeeding Mom

If breastfeeding is the direction you are led, we have some tips to offer that may aid you in your journey. From the foundational importance of praying through your feeding trials and triumphs, to the planning and products that can help ease your mind and preserve your sanity, these are some things we wish we had been told as mothers-to-be.

Prayer

We are convinced that there is no aspect of parenting that is beyond the Father's scope of wisdom or concern. And in a culture where the opinions of others can be overwhelming, we have seen that sometimes in the cacophony of voices deliberating, analyzing, and proselytizing the breast versus bottle question, we as Christian women may neglect to listen intently to the one Voice who is able to speak absolute truth into our lives, our families, and our circumstances.

As believers, we know we can call upon and rely on the prompting of the Spirit within us in each decision we are called to make. And yet, don't we often tend to compartmentalize the topics in which we feel God would be interested in providing direction? Ministry opportunity? Yes. Marriage partner? You bet. A move to a new community or new church? Certainly. Homeschool, private school, or public school? Absolutely.

Breast feed or bottle feed my baby? Well, see, my pediatrician says … but this magazine says … and my best friend told me … and my grandmother's advice was … and the La Leche League leader said …

Why do we do this? Do we believe there are aspects of daily life in which God is simply uninterested? Would it feel silly to make the question of whether or not to breastfeed a matter of prayer?

We need to seek the Spirit's leading for our family, and for each child, before we listen and give heed to any other voice in this matter. Jesus told us the Spirit would guide our steps.

> *"But when he, the Spirit of truth comes, he will guide you into all truth." (John 16:13, NIV)*

All truth. The Truth that surpasses any wisdom of man and the Truth that speaks to every situation. Later, the Apostle John would write to the new church:

> *"As for you, the anointing (referring to the anointing of the Spirit) you received from him remains in you, and you do not need anyone to teach you. **But as his anointing teaches you about all things and as that anointing is real, not counterfeit** - just as it has taught you, remain in Him" (1 John 2:27, NIV, emphasis ours).*

In context, of course, John was writing to the new believers to remind them that they need not make themselves susceptible to erroneous teachings because they thought themselves to be uneducated in God's truth. John is reminding them that the Spirit dwelling within them was enough to educate and enlighten them of the truth of God and His Word. God's wisdom is enough to speak and teach us truth in any and every circumstance in our lives ... including the decision of how we, as mothers, choose to feed the little ones He entrusts to us.

To those struggling with the initial breast vs. bottle decision, the Counselor can bring clarity. To those stuck at a difficult juncture, He can bring wisdom. To those mourning a breastfeeding journey that did not end well, He can bring comfort.

Perspective

As rewarding as the breastfeeding experience can be, there is also an element that calls for great sacrifice, particularly if your nursing baby won't take a bottle from you or anyone else. It's hard to be the sole source of nourishment in those early days, to arrange your schedule and your life so that you're never separated from your little one for too long a period. It is wearying to be the only one who can soothe and comfort her in the middle of the night. Sharing your body so consistently with someone else can take its toll.

What ministered to us most mightily in those moments of weariness and exhaustion was the perspective of viewing breastfeeding as a worshipful act of servanthood. In the moments when our own bodies were providing life and sustenance to our little ones, there was a communion with God, the Giver and Sustainer of life. When breastfeeding felt like more of a sacrifice than we were able to offer, we sensed the presence of Christ, redeeming our struggle by reminding us that we are never more like Him than when we are serving others. At the end of long days when we felt touched out and literally drained, the rescuing power of the Holy Spirit was the only thing that brought rejuvenation.

May the perspective that breastfeeding reveals the glory of God's creation while providing an incredibly tangible picture of the way God parents us in our own spiritual growth be a guiding truth that encourages you, body and soul, in those moments when you are convinced that you'll never make it to the goal you had in mind.

People

New mothers often feel hesitant to ask for help. We want to look like we have it all together: the picture of parental competence. *Oh, thanks, but I've got this.* Life with an infant, however, is no time for unnecessary heroics. In fact, it can be a powerful opportunity to learn how to accept the service of others as you serve the needs of your baby. Here are some ways to lean on the love and support of a community while feeding your child.

Professionals

We would find it impossible to adequately sing the praises of certified lactation consultants as resources for new nursing mothers! These specially-trained medical professionals can help to get you started with breastfeeding, or provide assistance in overcoming difficulties faced at any point. For a mother whose baby doesn't seem to be gaining weight or is struggling to latch, scheduling an appointment with a lactation consultant can make a world of difference. It is far easier to perform a perfect cradle hold with the inanimate doll at prenatal breastfeeding class than it is to position a real, flailing limbed baby peacefully at your engorged breast and accomplish the proper feeding angle.

Your LC will be able to provide those "try tucking this arm" and "use another pillow here" tips that can make all the difference. She can keep track of your newborn's weight and give instruction on how to tell when they have fully emptied each breast of that rich full-fat hindmilk before moving on to the other. Breastfeeding is her specialty, and she can be a tremendous blessing to you if you encounter a road block along the way.

Support system

Having your spouse at your side during those first few weeks of feedings is tremendously important. This is one area where men can feel useless (for obvious reasons) and anxious over their inability to jump into the situation and provide a quick fix. Just being there, though, with words of encouragement, tall glasses of water, pillow adjustments, tickling the toes of a drowsy newborn who can't stay awake for a feeding, or picking him up for a mid-feed burp to give the exhausted mom a breather; there are many ways that Daddy can play a significant role in the nourishment of his child, while serving his wife in ways she will never forget.

Beyond the support of a husband, the support of friends and family members is invaluable. When people providing meals go out of their way to avoid foods that can upset a baby's tummy, it touches a new mama's heart. When grandmas make sure the cupboards and refrigerator are packed with lots of snacks (there is no hunger like the hunger of a mama making milk around the clock), there is tangible love wrapped up in every granola bar. When friends don't bat an eyelash when baby needs to nurse in the middle of a conversation (or Bible study), it feels so safe and welcoming to the mother who desperately doesn't want to miss out on time and conversation with grown-ups.

Before the baby arrives, be praying that God would build a network of encouragement around you. And when people who love you ask how they can be of help during this overwhelming period of adjustment, please don't hesitate to give them suggestions! While it may be true that you are the one person who can breastfeed your baby, there are many ways to build a beautiful community of support that will hold you up and hold you close.

Preparation

While pre-planning can't always condition you to sail through every breastfeeding challenge with ease, there are a few ways to get a head start and increase your chances for a smoother start.

Take a Class

In any new venture, knowledge of the basic foundations and an understanding of potential obstacles will give you an advantage from the start. Many hospitals, as well as programs such as WIC, offer classes on introduction to breastfeeding, with nurses on hand to give a rundown of excellent information. While it's impossible to prepare for every possible scenario, having a solid grasp on foremilk vs. hindmilk and the different ways to position baby for feeding (football hold? who knew?) can make a big difference in the first few weeks.

Consider a Six-Week Goal

One of the most important pieces of practical wisdom we would offer the nursing mother is the common advice of trying to make it through six weeks. The first month-and-a-half is the hardest part of the breastfeeding journey. By far. The good news is that the vast majority of those initial struggles have tapered off and evened out by the six week mark. It seems like an eternity when you are just in week one and you are leaking milk everywhere, re-latching the baby every few minutes and the thought of your next nursing session makes you cringe. But then after a few weeks your nipples sort of toughen up, your milk supply evens out, your little one is eating more efficiently, and one day you discover you are starting to feel normal again.

Try to prepare yourself to persevere – if at all possible – through those first six weeks without making any major decisions about whether to continue beyond that point. You may be surprised at the change in perspective!

When I finally gave in and let myself not deem my worth
on my baby's breastfeeding ability and supplemented with
a few bottles here and there, it clicked. And six weeks
was the magical time frame; it just finally worked and we
never looked back! - Misty, Tennessee

Products

The baby aisles are stacked with all sorts of supplies to aid in breastfeeding. While different products work differently for each person, here are some that we found especially helpful.

Lanolin Cream

For those mamas who experience the often-intense discomfort of cracked, sore nipples, lanolin cream can be a $10 miracle-in-a-tube.

Nursing Pads

You may leak milk. You may leak a lot of milk. You may leak milk all the way through your bra and t-shirt while in the checkout line at Target. (Not that this purely hypothetical situation has ever happened to either of us. Ahem.) Breast pads provide both comfort and reassurance, particularly during the early weeks.

Nursing Camis or Covers

If you plan to breastfeed in public or around other people, a good nursing cover can give you a more discreet option. And for those new mothers who are not over-eager to share their post-partum midsections with the entire local coffeehouse, wearing a nursing camisole underneath a shirt or sweater makes it easy to pull the top shirt up, the cami down, and have almost full coverage during those away-from-home feedings.

Breast Pump

Whether you have a baby who sometimes takes a bottle, or whether an overactive let-down or low milk supply has made some pre- or post-feeding expressing of milk necessary, a good, reliable breast pump can make a big difference. This is one product that we would suggest researching and scouting reviews of before your purchase. There are good pumps, and then there are those that would make even the most mild-mannered of women feel tempted to let loose with a barrage of choice expletives. When you find the right one, it can be a lifesaver, as well as help you store up some precious mama milk in the freezer for the future.

Making Peace with the Bottle

Sometimes, whether due to a low milk supply, latch issues, hour-long nursing sessions around the clock that don't allow time to tend to other needs, or other insurmountable road blocks, breastfeeding just doesn't work out. And for many mothers who had set their hearts on nursing their babies, this can be devastating.

> *I was determined to breastfeed, but try as I might, my milk never came in. Just a few ounces, but no let down. Ever. Turned out that I had a retained piece of placenta, which prevented the let down. I cried buckets and was so heartbroken until I decided to let it go at three weeks. Although I'm sad about not breastfeeding, I'm sadder about the fact that I spent the first few weeks of my little guy's life being incredibly depressed instead of soaking up every second. – Emily, Arkansas*

Other women, for a myriad of reasons, choose formula-feeding from the beginning. And many struggle to maintain peace amidst judgmental words and attitudes from people in their lives — even total strangers — who disagree with their decision.

To all of these mothers, we would like to offer words that you may not have heard often enough: *It is okay.* To the woman who dreamed of nursing her baby and sits brokenhearted with a bottle, grieving the best-laid plans gone awry, we know that your pain is intense. Do not hesitate to bring your wounds in prayer before your Heavenly Father, who intimately knows your heart and desires to bring healing and redemption. And please know this: *You have not failed.*

To the mom who has weathered the stinging comments from those who have not walked in her shoes, we know that words can leave scars. Breathe deep the knowledge that a prayerfully-made decision means that *you have heeded His wisdom for your family.*

When it comes down to it, the most important aspect of feeding your baby is *that you feed your baby.* The method of delivery doesn't matter as much as the mindset of the mother. Our babies are delivered to us with an utter inability to feed themselves, and it requires an act of service on our parts every time we warm up a bottle or unsnap a nursing bra. With every hunger cue, we have the opportunity to stop whatever it is we are doing and participate in the miracle of nurturing life.

Providing your baby with life-giving nourishment is one of the most rewarding aspects of serving your baby in that first year because the results are so very tangible. When you are tenderly packing up those itty bitty baby clothes long since outgrown, you'll maybe cry a little, but you'll definitely experience a sense of accomplishment in knowing your willingness to serve has resulted in all that mind-boggling growth that marks the first year. Whether with breast, bottle, or both, you have served your baby well.

> *I had an absolutely horrible time with breastfeeding. After eight weeks of pure hades and a baby who kept losing weight, my husband told me that I had made it an idol,*

and needed to stop. God spoke through him, the baby got fat and happy on Enfamil, and I finally began to enjoy motherhood.

Nursing and all the other "perfect motherhood" standards we place upon ourselves are not what define our "success" as mothers. I have learned many more times since then that motherhood frequently involves letting our ideas and pride die to the needs of our children - even and especially when it goes against our best laid plans! - Missy, Texas

When I had my third child, I quickly became pregnant with my fourth. Despite trying everything, I simply was not meeting my child's needs through breastfeeding ...it was so emotionally difficult to realize this, and to transition to formula when my baby was six months old. But even then God was reminding me that He was providing for my baby. I was not my baby's ultimate Source ... God is. That whole process had a lot more prayers ... "God, why aren't I good enough? Why can't my body do this?" And God reminded me that it wasn't about me being perfect, it was about being made perfect in Him. - Grace, Mississippi

A word, too, to all of us, as a global sisterhood of mothers: let us carefully choose our words and our attitudes toward one another. Breastfeeding advocacy has done valuable work in educating and assisting women to make informed decisions. Far too often though, advocates have expressed their passions in ways that inflict guilt and pain on their formula-feeding friends and neighbors. Could we choose to be slow to speak and quick to listen?

The tearful mom across from you, is she asking for advice in wading through the nursing complications she is desperate to overcome?

Or is she, through her tears, asking for permission to let go of a difficult breastfeeding journey with peace, supported by friends who remind her of the incredible mother she is, regardless of how her baby is fed? Our words have such power, and our support and prayers for one another can help to illuminate the joys of motherhood, inspire the strength to get through, and point each hurt back to the healing grace of our Father.

I live in an area where it is assumed one will breastfeed if at all possible. All during my pregnancy, I read up on the benefits of both natural labor and breastfeeding, and I was prepared and excited for both.

I ended up with an emergency C-section at 33 weeks, and because my daughter was so premature, she couldn't latch properly. I pumped furiously for the first several weeks, ecstatic at being able to do one simple gesture to help my baby. Three weeks later I woke up to find I couldn't pump a single ounce. I did everything prescribed for a week, praying and crying and pleading with God. But I was completely dry. My lactation consultant finally told me kindly, "I think you might need to accept that this part of your journey is finished."

Another dream of mine died, and I felt the loss keenly every feeding, especially when we started venturing out into public. Ashamed of my failure, I assumed every mother around was judging me for not breastfeeding.

I eventually realized that my experience happened for a reason, and part of that reason was to help me be a less judgmental parent myself. I am thankful for the opportunities I have had to become a more empathetic friend and mother. And I have a beautiful, smart, joyous little toddler to whom I am completely bonded. God is good, and uses all things for His glory. – DLM, Portland

Our Breastfeeding Stories Revisited

As this chapter opened, we told you of the frustration, anxiety, and confusion that accompanied the beginning of our experiences in breastfeeding. Thankfully, the stories did not end there.

For Megan, I was determined to power through the early obstacles to nursing my baby, and in the beginning, that was exactly what I did. Through sheer determination mixed with the fear of no alternative, we made it through those milk-saturated, tearful earliest weeks. And I will say to this day that it was not blissful or ethereal. It was hard.

But day by day it got easier, and one day I realized I no longer gritted my teeth and gripped the nursing pillow when my milk let down. And then another day I realized I could nurse my baby in public without making a milky spectacle of us both. And then months down the road, I could do it all with my eyes closed – literally.

Dacey weaned when she was ready, right before her 2nd birthday. I was pregnant with Aliza Joy and my milk was drying up. We were done and we were both ready for that day. And when our AJ arrived, she latched on like a champ and we were both old pros right from the start. I remember looking down at her in our hospital bed as she latched on for the first time and just being overwhelmed once again with the wonder of it all. It was blissful and it was ethereal, and I was redeemed.

And for Laura, one afternoon, when Maya was around four months old, I gathered her into my arms for a pre-nap feeding. The house was quiet, and as my gaze fell onto my daughter's face, my heart swelled suddenly with the realization that I felt peace. Gone was the tension, gone were the tears. Even with that plastic shield still there as a reminder of our struggles, I was no longer preoccupied with its presence. The knowledge that another feeding was likely to come in a few short hours, and that I had just allowed my baby to pacify herself to sleep at my breast did not bother me in that moment. As I gave thanks to God in silent, joyful prayer, He touched my heart with a clear reminder that He was guiding me as I cared for her.

It was a revelation that took some time to bud and grow within me throughout the spring months, but I began to see the whole journey with new eyes. I gradually grew to recognize that the source of my anxiety came only from comparing my baby with others and my breastfeeding experience with what I perceived as the norm. Maya's frequent feedings caused me no fear until someone else implied that they should. Conversely, when I chose to focus simply on what I felt in my heart that my child needed, I felt peace—the perfect peace that comes from a steadfast trust in the One who placed her in my arms (Isaiah 26:3).

Though my perspective would often falter and anxiety would threaten to creep back in from time to time, the spring of Maya's first year of life was when I truly became her mother.

Six months after our first tear-filled night in the hospital, Maya began to nurse un-aided by the breast shield. I remember laughing aloud, thrilled at her accomplishment and amused by the thought that *isn't this just like God*? To bring me to a place of peace and trust in the face of struggle before removing that struggle from my life? Joy and awe. And now that we had made it this far—might as well try for a year?

In a precious twist of irony, we weren't even done at one year. My pre-baby insistence that I would never nurse a child who could walk up to me to feed flew out the window when Maya walked at eight months of age. Walk up, she did! And I didn't mind a bit. Her first birthday came and went, both of us still treasuring our morning and evening nursing sessions. It just wasn't time to be done. I didn't let many friends know that we were continuing on, but I had connected with a group of mamas in an online community in the meantime, many of whom were breastfeeding beyond a year. I drew some valuable camaraderie from them, as well as the confidence that I wasn't a complete wacko.

Finally, just after Maya's second birthday, we were done. Walking out of her room after goodnight kisses and what I knew would be our last time nursing, I sat down once again on the couch with Mark and cried. This time, though, I smiled through my tears. The man who had once spoken such vital encouragement to me to keep it up for six weeks now hugged me as I celebrated a breastfeeding journey that had spanned two whole years.

God knew all along. In the days before giving birth, when I barely gave breastfeeding a second thought, He knew that it would be my biggest parenting struggle in that first year, as well as one of the most vivid examples in my life of something that drew me closer to Him and taught me about serving through hardship. It was in the heavy shadow that I learned to cling to Him, trust that the Spirit was leading — even leading me outside the popular advice, and put one trembling foot in front of the other to follow.

In *One Thousand Gifts*, Ann Voskamp writes, "Dark is the holiest ground, the glory passing by. In the blackest, God is closest, at work, forging His perfect and right will. Though it is black and we can't see and our world seems to be free-falling and we feel utterly alone, Christ is most present to us, I-beam supporting in earthquake."[8]

Winter to spring. Tears to laughter. Intense defeat to sweet reward. All glory to He who fills us with "all joy and peace as [we] trust in him, so that [we] may overflow with hope by the power of the Holy Spirit." (Romans 15:13, NIV)

As I fed her, He fed me.

---

8   Ann Voskamp, *One Thousand Gifts: A Dare to Live Fully Right Where You Are* (Grand Rapids: Zondervan, 2011) 156.

Closing Thoughts on Feeding

Spirit-led parenting is not contingent upon any certain methodology. It's about recognizing your child's uniqueness, as our Father recognizes ours, and responding to each challenge under His constant guidance.

- As you partner with God in the miracle of growing new life, don't neglect to desperately seek His truth for the direction He would have you take. (And this holds true if the new baby is your first or fifth! What worked — or didn't work — with one child will not always be the same with the next.)

- As that little one grows and the time comes to start thinking about starting solid foods, may we not forget to once again seek God's direction on when to introduce them to the bounty of foods He created to nourish and sustain us.

- As our children continue to grow, may we never minimize the importance of seeking His guidance in what we provide as nutrition for the little bodies growing up in our homes.

We know how very easy it is to allow the jumble of voices that speak to this topic to be given such volume that His still small voice is nearly silenced. Let us never lose the wonder of being loved by a God who has wisdom to offer for every single aspect of our lives. The God of the universe is intimately invested in the choices we make as parents, and He has a word for you. May each of us be desperate for His truth in the day we need it, and may we have the courage to trust His leading and direction, knowing that no one on the planet loves these little ones He has chosen us to care for more than He.

Chapter Five

As They Sleep

-Megan's Story-

Before I became a mother, before I knew the intense and primal call to protect and nurture that is triggered by hearing your baby cry, when the author of a parenting book suggested that babies might cry for up to 45 minutes while being trained to sleep independently, it seemed reasonable to me. Not something I was excited about, but it sounded workable. And actually, in my first readings of his advice, I kind of brushed all of the techniques he described to the side because I was fairly confident God was going to send us a baby who loved to sleep.

I had no idea at the time what giving my infant the gift of sleep would cost me, or what it would cost her.

For the first two weeks of Dacey's life, she slept and nursed and slept and nursed, just the way most newborns do. I held her a lot and marveled over the wonder of it all. What I didn't fully realize was that beyond the normal sleepy patterns of a newborn, Dacey was sleeping a lot due to the influence of the many medications I was given during her delivery, as well as the pain medication I was taking to manage the pain of her Caesarean birth. My mother-in-law had been staying with us to ease the transition and help me recover, and on the very day she left, Dacey woke up to the world and began to resist the neat, tidy, and uncomplicated schedule I had been instructed to have her follow.

The weeks that passed from the day she turned two weeks old until about her fourth or fifth month of life were long, dark, desperate days for me. For every "your baby should," I was faced with a "my baby doesn't." Nearly every baby expert was insistent that babies be taught from day one to fall asleep independently, on their own, with no "sleep props," no intervention or involvement from a parent, no rocking chairs gliding baby off to sleep, no walking the halls with baby bouncing gently in the arms. Those were all dangerous habits to form, they said, because those habits would all have to be broken at some point to get baby to go to sleep on her own. And that was, after all, the main goal a parent should be working towards accomplishing.

Not only did my first child not buy into the concept of independent sleep fresh from the womb, she also had no desire to sleep the full hour and a half to two hour stretch at each of her daytime naps. This caused great and perplexing problems for me, because every single one of the "suggested schedules" in the baby-management books I read hinged on these long, leisurely naps. At each nap, she slept exactly forty-five minutes. The books suggested solutions for this problem; one author suggested I pick her up if she cried, then lay her back down when she stopped crying. If she started crying when laid down, the book said, I was to pick her up again until she stopped, and then lay her back down. Over and over. And over.

"If it takes fifty or one hundred times, or even 150, surely you're prepared to do that in order to teach your baby to sleep and to get your own time back, aren't you, luv?"[9]

You can imagine how physically exhausting this became. Another book instructed me to let the baby cry through this wake-up period, assuming the crying would wear baby out, and she would fall back to sleep. I gave that a try a time or two, but as I shared in the opening chapter, I could not follow through with this method. Hearing my baby cry hysterically for me aroused such an overwhelming physical reaction within me (my heart would race, I would sweat, I couldn't concentrate on anything) that I simply could not ignore her cries.

So for those first five months or so, she wouldn't fall asleep on her own, she wouldn't nap as long as she was "supposed to," and she most definitely, absolutely, was not sleeping through the night. For a first-time mom who had been assured by several different resources that the key to good nighttime sleep was a good daytime schedule, this caused no small amount of frustration. Nothing I did could "fix" her daytime nap schedule, and I was just sure this was the stumbling block to good ten-hour stretches of sleep at night.

For those first months of my daughter's life, I awakened each morning with a pit in my stomach, a lingering dread that I could not shake. Each new sunrise meant another day filled with sleep journals and doing battle with my tiny baby over sleep.

-Laura's Story-

I love to sleep. I mean, I don't just enjoy it; I need it, crave it, and turn into someone not-so-nice when I haven't had enough of it. In

---

9   Tracy Hogg and Melinda Blau, *The Baby Whisperer Solves All Your Problems* (New York: Atria Books 2005) 223

our pre-children days, I enjoyed nothing more than lounging lazily in bed throughout the morning hours, often rising just in time to start thinking about lunch. So a major anxiety for me after finding out we were going to be parents was how on earth I was going to function with less sleep.

Sure enough, it hit me like a Mack truck nine months later when our sweet newborn girl introduced me to hours of the morning that I hadn't known existed. As I said in the last chapter, Maya ate so frequently that my nights were full of feedings, and her naps were far more brief than I'd expected, based upon the books. I distinctly remember sitting bleary-eyed at a breastfeeding support group for new moms and pulling out a list of questions that I had brought along. At the top of the list was the only question that really mattered to me at the time. It said, in bold, desperately-scrawled letters, "When do I get to sleep again???" I posed that question to the lactation consultant who had greeted me at the door. She laughed pleasantly, gave me a pat on the shoulder, and continued with her advice on getting a good latch. "Wait!" I interrupted, tersely. "You did not answer my question!" I think I might have scared her.

The first several weeks I got through on pure adrenaline. But by the time Maya was a few months old, I found myself sitting in my darkened living room, feeding her for the second or third time that night, and peering out at the other houses on my block. "I am the only one awake," I lamented. "I want to cry." And often, I did.

What was making the nights so hard for me, though, wasn't so much the reduced sleep. That was frustrating, for sure. But the main source of my frustration was this nagging fear that something was wrong. That I was failing somehow, that my daughter was abnormal. If you're a mom or a mom-to-be, you know that (as Megan said) the vast majority of the advice you receive at first (whether solicited or otherwise) tends to center around sleep. And from what I was hearing, I should most definitely expect my three-month-old to be sleeping through the night.

We read the books. Our babies do not.

The one issue that drives parents and parents-to-be to turn to the advice of experts, more than any other, is the matter of infant sleep. At the time of this writing, a search on Amazon.com for the keywords "baby sleep" yields more than twenty results for books centered exclusively on this topic! There is an entire industry devoted to coaching parents through the process of helping their little ones to sleep through long, restful naps and wonderfully uninterrupted nights.

Our earliest experiences with our first babies were heavily influenced by many of these popular parenting books all devoted to the necessity of sleep training. These books are popular for a reason: **sleep deprivation is a very real thing and the allure of consistent nighttime sleep for a baby as early as six weeks is hard to deny.** No sane person wants to endure the physical toll of sleepless nights for months or years on end, and so the draw to stop sleep problems before they start is a strong one. Most of these books, however, encourage parents to foster independent sleep by using some form of the same method: leaving baby alone to cry — a practice referred to in parenting circles as "cry-it-out sleep training."

Cry-it-out is based on the premise that once babies reach a certain age or weight, they are developmentally ready to sleep long stretches of time without any intervention from a care giver. Some books suggest that babies as young as six weeks old are ready for independent nighttime sleep, while other books suggest waiting until four or six months of age to implement this practice.

As new parents, we poured over these books, and the logic of it made sense on the surface. Sleep is a good and vital part of life, something created by God as a way for our bodies and our minds to find healing and restoration. In some Christian parenting circles (including the ones we traveled in as new moms), cry-it-out sleep training is very much the norm for parenting a new baby. Because it is a practice that is so normal and encouraged in parenting culture, both of us believed it was the right and only way to approach sleep with our new babies.

You can imagine our confusion—and later, despair—when attempting to implement this approach only led to significant internal conflicts. Megan spent day after day and night after night trying desperately to remain strong and follow the path that made sense, the approach that worked for others, the right way to do things. Yet she was deeply troubled in her spirit as she listened to Dacey crying, sensing in her heart that the one thing her daughter needed was the comforting presence of a parent. As Laura wrote about in her opening story, she wrestled so much with the idea of sleep training that she couldn't even bring herself to attempt it with Maya when the time came, leading to feelings of guilt and failure right from the start.

What we didn't know at the time was that other parents experienced the same tension in trying to implement an approach that they had been taught was the right way. Friends and readers of our blogs have shared stories with us, assuring us that we weren't alone in our feelings of failure:

> *We had several friends at church and couples we respected*
> *that were taking parenting classes. I read parts of the*
> *material from the parenting class offered at our church,*
> *and it all sounded so simple. And it was 'God's Way.'*
> *But it didn't work. I couldn't make it work. And I began*

to wonder if I couldn't do something as simple as get a baby to sleep, how could I do the really big stuff? How could I possibly point him to Christ? I was convinced Eli would go to Hell because I couldn't get him to follow the schedule laid out in the book. – Jenny, Oklahoma

When my oldest son was four months old, I started the cry-it-out routine. I did it half-heartedly at first, hoping he wouldn't need too much crying. But he did cry, and when I would go in to check him every five minutes, he only got more frantic. One night, I was feeling like an absolute failure as a mother and determined that tonight would be the night that he fell asleep by himself. He cried for 45 minutes until I went in, picked up the slobbery sobbing baby, sobbed myself, calmed him, nursed him, and threw the book away. I decided that if that's what being a good mom entailed, I wanted no part of it. – April, Texas

Those first six weeks with our first baby are a blur of tears of frustration and anger because I could NOT get my baby on any sort of schedule, and he refused to do anything that the book said he should or would. I remember distinctly when he was six or eight weeks old, I yelled at him because he woke up ninety minutes after eating and wanted to nurse again. Based on the book's advice, I should have just left him there to cry, because it wasn't time for him to eat again, so I tried it. I put him in his bassinet and let him cry ... and thought I was going to throw up.

After that, I gave up on the book and just accepted that I was a failure of a mom and obviously just didn't have it in me to be a disciplined person who could get a baby on a schedule. I really and truly felt like a complete and

utter failure, and blamed myself for my son's sleeping
and eating habits, but I knew I couldn't keep following
the 'schedule' the book had told me would work. - Kate,
Illinois

Reading through the stories of other Christian parents who were led to believe this is the right or godly way to parent a new baby, one might get the impression that *all* Christian parenting circles heavily emphasize this approach, but that would be a huge overgeneralization. We've spoken with many Christian parents who had never heard of any of the books that held so much sway over us as new parents. It seems that the cultural climate of where a person lives and worships determines what approaches to parenting are popular at any moment in time. The fact remains, though, that in many areas of the country these methods of working with infant sleep issues are the accepted norm among followers of Christ.

So what makes this don't-spoil-the-baby, cry-it-out, tough-love philosophy so desirable in certain Christian parenting cultures?

Understanding Realistic Expectations for Infant Sleep

A key component of much of the literature given to new parents who are Christian is the idea that every aspect of the new baby's life must be parent-directed. The subtle implication throughout the book is that it is the parents' responsibility to teach the baby who is boss from day one and that the needs of the family supersede the baby's needs, therefore, the parent directs all decisions about sleep, feeding, and schedule for the greater good of the family. On the surface, who could argue with this? What these books fail to take into account, however, are the very real developmental needs of little ones in that first year of life.

Here is some data on infant sleep that we were ignorant of as we rocked our babies through the nights, hearts aching because our daughters weren't "normal."

- Medical professionals consider "sleeping through the night" to be a five-hour stretch, generally in the hours from midnight to five a.m.[10]

- Breast milk is digested by a baby's body in two hours or less. [11]

- According to one longitudinal study, at the age of six months, only 16% of babies were sleeping ten or more hours without waking at night. [12]

- Another study reported that at twelve months, 50% of children still woke at least once per night.[13]

- Even children who have been sleeping five or more hours per night may relapse into frequent nighttime waking due to teething, illness, gastric reflux or other gastrointestinal issues, or preparing to reach a new developmental milestone. [14]

None of this information was included in the baby care books we read that advocated cry-it-out sleep training. We also find it extremely puzzling that material written with a Christian parenting audience in mind fails to recognize that nighttime wake-ups may very well be part of God's design for the newborn baby.

---

10   Elizabeth Pantley, *The No-Cry Sleep Solution* (New York: McGraw Hill) 50-51

11   Kelly Bonyata, "Increasing Low Milk Supply," [Internet – WWW, URL] http://kellymom.com/bf/supply/low-supply.html, 13 May 1998

12   "Studies on Normal Infant Sleep," [Internet – WWW, URL] http://www.kellymom.com/parenting/sleep/sleepstudies.html

13   Ibid

14   Ibid

Consider what Dr. William Sears says of frequent waking for babies:

Nightwaking has survival benefits. In the first few months, babies' needs are the highest, but their ability to communicate their needs is the lowest. Suppose a baby slept deeply most of the night. Some basic needs would go unfulfilled. Tiny babies have tiny tummies, and mother's milk is digested very rapidly. If a baby's stimulus for hunger could not easily arouse her, this would not be good for baby's survival. If baby's nose was stuffed and she could not breathe, or was cold and needed warmth, and her sleep state was so deep that she could not communicate her needs, her survival would be jeopardized.

One thing we have learned during our years in pediatrics is that babies do what they do because they're designed that way. In the case of infant sleep, research suggests that active sleep protects babies. Suppose your baby sleeps like an adult, meaning predominantly deep sleep. Sounds wonderful! For you, perhaps, but not for baby. Suppose baby had a need for warmth, food, or even unobstructed air, but because he was sleeping so deeply he couldn't arouse to recognize and act on these needs. Baby's well-being could be threatened. It appears that babies come wired with sleep patterns that enable them to awaken in response to circumstances that threaten their well-being. We believe, and research supports, that frequent stages of active (REM) sleep serve the best physiologic interest of babies during the early months, when their well-being is most threatened.[15]

---

15   William Sears, "Eight Infant Sleep Facts Every Parent Should Know," [Internet – WWW, URL] http://askdrsears.com/topics/sleep-problems/8-infant-sleep-facts-every-parent-should-know

If night waking is absolutely common for infants, it seems to make sense that this is part of God's design for the health and well-being of babies during this phase of life. It is completely understandable that parents want to avoid or lessen the effects of being up at night with little ones, but if we view this moment in time as a normal and passing phase, it helps the sacrifice of sleep to be a little more tolerable.

Unfortunately, neither of us were encouraged with these facts about infant sleep when we were brand-new parents. From parenting books to the Internet articles to the advice of friends, the mantra we heard was: *sleep at all cost.*

The voices speaking into our lives as we weathered those first months of parenting spoke so often of "you have to be tough" and "turn off the baby monitor and get your sleep" and "solid daytime schedules build solid nighttime sleep" that it never occurred to us that we were missing the bigger picture. Megan worked tirelessly on those sleep journals, obsessively focused on solving Dacey's sleep problems while Laura dodged questions about how Maya was sleeping at night; yet neither of us had truly tuned in to the movement in our spirits that wouldn't allow us to leave our babies to cry in their cribs.

The Revelation

How did we go from feeling miserable over the matter of sleep to embracing a concept known as nighttime parenting?[16] On parallel paths, God led us to a new perspective and gave to each of us a different kind of gift.

For Megan, during the early months, the Lord provided me with a wonderful community of friends during my transition into

---

16   "nighttime parenting" is a phrase coined by Dr. William Sears in his book *The Baby Book* (Boston: Little, Brown, and Company)

motherhood. Every week, we would gather to drink coffee and share prayer requests while our little ones played. One week, I was feeling particularly discouraged with our struggles with sleep, and I shared with the group that my prayer request for that week was for wisdom and rest. I remember very vividly that I was holding Dacey (she was about five months at the time) and complaining about all the time we were spending in the rocking chair.

Everyone listened sympathetically. The mom sitting next to me that morning was a woman who had a beautiful little boy, but who was also in the middle of a long, painful journey to have a second child, a journey that had been marked by many losses and heartbreaks. She gently remarked that if she had known at the time that their little boy might be the only child they would be able to have, she would have been happy to spend a lot more time in the rocking chair with him, enjoying and relishing his babyhood.

I don't know if I've ever told her how powerful that insight was to me. That day, in that circle of friends, God opened my eyes, heart, and mind to what I was losing out on. As I drove home, He reminded me that not only was I not guaranteed to be able to have more babies after this one, I wasn't even guaranteed that I would have tomorrow with this baby. What would be so wrong, really, with actually enjoying the closeness and bonding time that so much time in the rocking chair was creating between my daughter and me?

My friend's remark allowed me the freedom to explore parenting philosophies beyond the confines of the books I had buried my nose in for months. Prior to that time, I was very close-minded to alternative approaches because I had been led to believe that other parenting philosophies created spoiled, unpleasant, manipulative children and sacrificed the marital relationship by emphasizing the bond between child and parents. I had been hesitant to acknowledge that if sleep training wasn't working for us, it was okay! Perhaps my baby actually needed me to attend to her needs, she was not being manipulative, and I could go to her when she cried and not worry about being a bad mother.

For Laura, somewhere amidst the long days and nights spent worrying over my mothering failures and my daughter's sleep "issues", I began to experience occasional glimmers of peace. It was not a peace that made sense, as at that point I lacked both the knowledge I now have about normal infant sleep patterns and the perspective of hindsight. No, this was as clear an example as I had ever had of a peace that passes understanding. Slowly but surely, those glimmers became more prominent moments of the Holy Spirit leading me through my fears and teaching me to trust in Him. I began to perceive and understand that my daughter was exhibiting neither behavioral nor physiological issues by waking for food or comfort during the night. I was not doing anything wrong by responding when those needs arose. I found staggeringly sweet relief in those revelations.

Most freeing, though, in this journey was the realization that I wasn't letting God down by turning my back on the idea of sleep-training. I wasn't making a decision that stood at odds with doing things His way. In fact, it was His very voice that had guided me through the turmoil of confusion and guilt to the place of peace. It was His hand that pointed me in the direction of the instincts He had placed inside me the moment my daughter was placed in my arms. His Spirit had comforted and reassured me when I questioned the decisions we were making. I was beginning to feel quite strongly that the Lord Himself had guided me towards the path of tending to and serving our daughter in the nighttime parenting hours.

His Perfect Example

As time passed, both of us gradually began to understand that God parents us perfectly. *Perfectly.* He never errs in the way He expresses His love towards us. He doesn't simply "manage" us, but tends to us in our need. While there is no doubt that He challenges us, instructs us, and expects growth in our lives as we follow Him, it is with a gentle, ever-present, reassuring love that He frames those lessons. He is unceasingly patient, and never expects more of us than we are capable of demonstrating.

Such steadfast, tireless devotion flies in the face of what our current society tells us: that we are entitled to view each venture we undertake with an end goal of convenience. In truth, our roles as parents do not end in late evening and pick up again when the sun rises. The way we parent our children at night is just as crucial to their development as the way we parent them during the daytime hours.

An interesting picture of how this plays out in relationship comes to us in the second chapter of the Gospel of John, when Nicodemus came to Jesus in the night. He is wrestling with his budding belief and lingering doubts, yet he was not turned away by Jesus because his need came at an inconvenient hour. Jesus recognized the infancy of Nicodemus' faith and met with him, offering explanation, instruction, and answers in that encounter which came under cover of darkness.

This nighttime meeting shaped and deepened Nicodemus' faith so significantly that a short time later, in his next mention in scripture, we see him speaking out among his fellow Pharisees in Christ's defense. And in his final appearance, in John 19, he has come full circle, publicly showing his devotion to Jesus by joining with Joseph of Arimathea in retrieving and burying Christ's crucified body. The transformation of his character did not come out of a teaching he witnessed during one of Christ's addresses to the masses, but rather in a one-on-one conversation with the Lord in an unplanned meeting in the tender hours of the night.

It's not uncommon for people to share stories of God speaking to them in the still of the night. For Megan, one of the most vivid remembrances of God meeting me in the night was when I was in college. My heart had been broken by someone, and I found myself completely alone on my dorm floor. I poured out my heart to Him in tears and sobs, and to this day, I can remember how He seemed to fill the concrete block walls with His comforting presence. In that moment I knew without a doubt that I could trust Him to heal my brokenness.

Could it be that the time we spend caring for our children in those dark, quiet hours have more impact than we realize in shaping their security, trust, and confidence in us? And that such deepening of our relationship with them could be an incredible asset as we seek to guide them, with God's help, to new levels of emotional and spiritual growth in the future?

It's hard for us to answer those questions definitively. Our children may have grown beyond the baby years, but we are still in the trenches of daily parenting, and we are still seeking God's guidance in raising them in love, wisdom, and knowledge of Him. But we have to think there must be something to the picture our Heavenly Father gives to us with His constant presence through His Spirit. That God would choose to model to us all-day and all-night parenting that never turns from one of His children in need … we think that speaks volumes about His plan for us as parents.

The Redemption

Learning to emulate God the Father while being motivated to serve like God the Son and living in step with God the Spirit — these are all powerful motivations to practice nighttime parenting. Yet God surprised both of us by illuminating another purpose to those lonely nights spent in the rocking chair. In fact, as we surrendered to His plan and purpose for those nighttime wake-ups, He turned around the frustration, tears, and despair by ministering to each of us in the most unexpected way.

For Megan, the nighttime parenting approach soothed my mind in that it allowed me to let go of the unrealistic expectation of uninterrupted nights, but it did little to meet my own personal and physical need for sleep. Although I understood why Dacey was waking so often at night, I still found myself grumbling and complaining about it. I would get cranky with her at night and snippy with my husband during the day.

I remember one particularly alarming incident that vividly illustrates my fatigue level at that time. Dacey was very high-needs and very unhappy when she wasn't with Mommy, so I rarely left the house alone. One afternoon, Kyle was home and I just needed to stop by the post office to buy stamps, so while Dacey napped, I slipped out of the house on my own. As I left the parking lot of the post office, I narrowly avoided a major collision with a semi-truck that had run a red light. Driving home more than a little shaken, my mind went to a dark place. For just a few minutes, I entertained the thought of how nice it would have been to be in an accident and taken to the hospital where I could at least get some sleep. *That* is how tired I was! I knew that even beyond the practical measures I would eventually employ to help with exhaustion, it wasn't enough. I had to make this a matter of prayer.

Here's what the Lord impressed on my heart: Since the day Dacey was born, my spiritual life had begun to atrophy. I was tired and not just a little distracted. My quiet time in the Scripture and in prayer took a backseat as I mostly focused on just surviving day-today. As I prayed over this matter of being up so much at night, the Lord gently prompted me to consider that if I was resolute in my decision to avoid cry-it-out sleep training, and if I was going to be up at night anyway, could I possibly conceive of the idea that these moments alone in the dark and quiet at night were *a gift from Him*? It was so difficult to carve out time alone with my God during the day. What if I flipped the attitude switch in my mind?

Rather than viewing these little interruptions at night as exhausting drudgery and empty sacrifice, perhaps I could use them as pockets of solitude for prayer and Scripture meditation.

This was an utterly radical concept to me, but I decided to go with it. I could always benefit from more Scripture memory, so I would meditate on Scripture I already knew or pick out new verses during the day and recite them to myself at night. Mostly though, I just prayed. Prayed for myself, for my husband, my daughter, my family, my friends, and anyone and everyone the Lord brought to mind.

The Lord richly and deeply rewarded the way I served my daughter in that time. I hadn't felt that connected to Him in a long, long time. Once she began sleeping longer stretches at night (and eventually through the night—no sleep training required!), my prayer life began to slack again. There was something about meeting the Lord in the absolute solitude of a quiet night that was profoundly productive and satisfying.

For Laura, looking back upon the sleepless nights of new motherhood, I remember the overwhelming fatigue and serious battles with bad attitudes. I remember the early mornings when my foggy mind would wonder how on earth I was going to make it through the day until bedtime. The nighttime hours that stretched on endlessly as every tick of the clock reminded me of the rest I was missing.

The pure grace in it all, though, is that what I remember far above everything else is simply how God met me there, pouring strength into my days and tucking peace around me through the watches of each night. Providing me with clear examples of His faithful provision and Father heart.

It is hard ... oh yes, it is ... for someone who treasures sleep as much as I do to count those weary months as gift. But had Maya been born one of those "good sleepers," or had I been able to follow through on my original sleep-training plan, I would have missed out on countless prayerful hours and precious moments of quiet. I've often heard it said that a baby who sleeps through the night is "such a blessing to her mama." I know now that I was blessed to be given a child who woke me up to what I truly needed.

The Spiritual Dimension of Nighttime Parenting

As we began to share our stories of spiritual growth on our blogs, we were wonderfully surprised to discover through the response of friends and readers that we weren't alone on this path of meeting God in the middle of the night, praying to the rhythm of the rocking chair:

> *I remember one night being up with my first son, when he was a few months old, and just being more tired than I thought was possible. I was actually weeping in frustration that his little eyes were wide open at some wee small hour of the morning. And something inside me (thank you, Holy Spirit) said, 'pray.' And I was too tired to scoff at the suggestion. And so I prayed. And there was peace. And some sort of contentment. – Kimberly, Virginia*

> *A few months ago when the lack of sleep started getting to me the Lord reminded me of something. I was reading a*

book about 'praying the hours' and I discovered that there are people out there who get up in the middle of the night (on purpose!) to 'pray the night watch.' I think about that as I'm up with my 15-month-old. I don't always pray, but it is a spiritual discipline that some people purposefully choose for years on end, and they don't even get the joy of a tired little bundle surrendering to sleep in their arms! – Amy, Idaho

I finally had that moment in the night where I realized that often it is the only time God can get my attention. Things are too noisy during the day for me to hear His still, small voice. Last night, as I was standing by Joshua's bed, I asked God to speak to me, and so many scriptures came to mind. It sometimes seems that I am only able to be reconnected with God during those middle-of-the-night moments. – Keri, Georgia

The redemptive work that God did in both of our lives in this area was a process of our continual surrender and His continual unfurling of beauty. He carried us through the initial tearful note-taking and self-doubt to the light bulb moments where we discovered new freedom in releasing our expectations and seeking His example and lead. Then, as a breathtaking bonus, He took our initial fears that we were failing to heed His ways, and shattered them by drawing each of us closer than ever to His heart. The nights that once held heartache now held the promise of peace and the comfort of communion with our Father.

Practical Solutions for Sleepless Nights

We hope that these stories from our own experiences and the stories of others are encouraging. We don't want, however, to ignore the fact that the physical toll from lost and broken sleep is a very, very real thing. No matter how spiritually rewarding it is to view nighttime parenting as a practice in spiritual discipline, week after week or month after month of not sleeping for solid stretches at night will affect quality of life during the day.

Sleep deprivation is awful. There's a reason it's used as torture: it's torturous! Not being able to sleep for at least four hours straight at night can make you feel like a zombie, stumbling through the days with a foggy, barely-functioning brain. Additionally, a lack of sleep can make you hyper-sensitive to emotions. Something that might feel like a minor upset under well-rested circumstances can feel like a complete and utter disaster from which you will never recover when you are operating on little sleep.

We have both noticed that weathering sleep deprivation was absolutely the hardest with our older children. Parenting our second children through the nights was somehow easier, and we've heard from parents of more than a few children that it gets easier with each new baby.

We'd also like to encourage you with some of the practical ways we survived those sleep-deprived days. Here is what has worked for us:

Leaning On Your Spouse

In the early newborn days, each of us found that while we were the sole source of nourishment for our babies, there were little acts of moral support that our husbands could provide that proved tremendously helpful: getting up alongside us at night, taking over diaper changes, and just generally *being there*. Over time, as we gained confidence and hit more of a groove, we found that those things weren't as crucial anymore, but other signs of partnership became more valuable.

Try taking advantage of a weekend morning, for instance, to place a wide-awake baby in Daddy's waiting arms when the sun comes up, so that Mommy can fall into bed for a couple more precious hours of sleep. On those rough nights where illness or other factors mean that the waking seems almost constant, he can take a shift — walking the floors, bouncing and humming, providing comfort while you soak up a little more rest. If baby has older siblings, perhaps put a system in place where, during the nighttime hours, your husband gets up with big brother or sister if they need the potty, a drink, etc., and you focus on tending to the little one. Teaming up on the nighttime parenting calls can make a huge difference!

Catching Up With the DVR

It would be great to say that every middle-of-the-night feeding lends itself perfectly to focused prayer or joyful awe of the miracle of life. Quite honestly, though, sometimes you just need a distraction at that hour to keep from melting into a pool of sorry whining and wallowing. (Or is that just us?) Why not keep a bunch of recorded shows on hand, particularly in those first several weeks when feedings tend to take a crazy-long time? If you're going to be up anyway, you might as well be catching up with 30 Rock. Laura is pretty sure she watched nearly an entire season of American Idol between the hours of 1:00 and 4:00 AM.

Looking Ahead

Another non-spiritual strategy to employ is to set a goal or incentive for yourself for the bleary-eyed day ahead. Whether it is the promise of a trip through the Starbucks drive-thru after a grocery run, or making a date with your husband to crash on the couch together after the kids are in bed that evening, it often helps to have a lovely little plan in front of you.

Early Bedtimes

If multiple nights of little sleep are starting to take their toll, perhaps work out an arrangement with your spouse where you go to bed nearly right after your baby, and your husband brings her to you a few hours later for a dream feed (rousing her from sleep just enough to nurse). You may hardly even wake up for that feeding, and he can then put her back down to sleep. Even though you may be up later in the night for another feeding, it could feel like far less of a physical drag if you can get some good, solid sleep earlier on. That evening time is so hard to give up, but even doing this two or three times a week can be a huge help in those hardest of months.

Naps

Some of us sleep easily during the daytime as adults, while others of us tend to wake up grumpy, groggy, disoriented, and basically a real joy to be around. But in the new-baby days, it really does help to try to sleep as much as possible, around-the-clock. Anyone with more than one child (particularly a non-napping child) knows that the "sleep when baby sleeps" advice really only works when you have just the one baby. Maybe Grandma and Grandpa, Auntie or Best Friend could come over to help when you absolutely must nap? If you can find a way to get some naps in, make an effort to receive daytime sleep as God's provision for your physical and emotional health.

Pursuing Perspective

This one is much easier to lean on with a second (or more)-born, as it's difficult to completely understand the concept during the first experience of newborn haze. Sitting in the nursery in the wee hours with our younger children, each of us often thought of our first babies sleeping soundly in the next room, no longer needing to be rocked or cuddled to sleep. In those moments, you can concentrate on two bittersweet truths: First, that these new baby days (and nights) do not last forever, and that there is more rest just around the corner. And second, that there is a part of you that will someday miss sitting in your cozy recliner in the nighttime stillness with a baby snuggled up in your arms.

Those babies dare to grow up and become more independent by the day. As much as we would like to fast-forward through the baby season of life when we are feeling foggy and sleep-deprived, it's such a short time in the Big Picture of parenting. Far too soon, we stand misty-eyed beside the big-kid bed, wishing there was a way to slow time's relentless march forward. Sometimes, remembering those things is enough to cause frustration to fizzle, and you may find yourself drawing your little one just a bit closer to you in that big chair, thanking God for the gift of that moment.

Prayer and Self-Care

Take a shower. Wear that skirt that makes you smile. Get lost in a book. Do something restorative and never feel guilty for practicing self-care. Most importantly, saturate your days and nights with prayer. Our friend Gretchen, a mother of eight, told us this is how she survives the sleepless season:

> *Every night, before I sleep, I pray to God that he will give me the sleep I need. Not want, or deserve or crave, but what I truly need. It does wonders for the days that follow.*

Reward Beyond Measure

We've shared a lot with you here on the topic of infant sleep. Again, there are (many) entire books filled with research, opinions and advice on this matter. Our intent has never been to persuade you that there is some sort of biblical mandate demanding that you approach sleep in a specific way. At the heart of our message about

Spirit-led parenting is the idea that God knows perfectly what will work within each family's unique blend of personalities and temperaments. It is completely within the parameters of Spirit-led parenting that your family's choices regarding infant sleep may very well look different than ours.

Many years have passed now since we first sat bleary-eyed in the night, stunned by how bewildering and confusing sleep had suddenly become. We've long since moved on from midnight visits to Google, asking it "why four month old no sleep night?" The painfully detailed sleep journals have been saved for posterity, not for reference. We don't just think differently about sleep now; we ourselves are different.

For in the practice of nighttime parenting, we allowed ourselves to be molded by God's ever-present hand. We believe the specific reason God led us to view nighttime with our babies differently is because as our Father, He wanted to attend to our specific needs in that moment in life. In the stillness of the night, as we fed our babies, He nourished us with His presence and His word. By the subtle glow of the night light as we changed diapers, He changed us, allowing us to see that through Him, we could be more than we ever thought we could be. As our feet tread miles of footfalls, muffled by carpet and *shhhhhhhh*, He sang over us words of comfort, hope and surrender.

The call to follow Christ is inextricably connected to the call to serve others in love. Who needs to experience the ministry of the body of Christ more than the insecure, the weak, and the helpless? Into our arms He delivers these new ones, and He is faithful to empower us to have all that we need to be His hands and feet to them. We gladly cling to the lessons learned to the rhythm of the rocking chair, for in that gentle, quiet place He carved into our hearts that the cost of serving is high, but the reward is the supernatural shaping of ourselves to become more like Him.

Chapter Six

As We Parent Together

Whether you've been married for a decade before children arrive or you decide to get married because baby is already on the way, becoming parents changes everything. Decades of daytime talk shows have capitalized on the reality that the changes parenting brings aren't always positive. "She loves the baby more than she loves me," and, "It was never like this before we had children," are thematic threads running through popular sitcoms, women's magazine articles, and hit movies. Infant-care manuals can drive the message deeper.

> *"Night-crying babies also can turn intimate, loving moments between a husband and wife into vague memories...The anger and isolation these parents feel starts because of a crying baby, but it often grows into serious marital problems."* [17]

The message seems clear enough: parenting brings change, and it's a change for the worse.

---

17   Charles E. Schaefer, Ph.D. and Michael R. Petronko, Ph.D., *Teach Your Baby to Sleep Through the Night* (New York: G.P. Putnam's Sons 1987) 41

As with most things unknown in life, worst-case scenarios collide with active imaginations, and we can quickly find ourselves painted into a fear-drenched corner. Both of us entered parenthood with the same primary fear: *What if having a baby changes my marriage?*

It wasn't all that long ago that each of us wrestled down these pre-parenting worries:

-*Megan's Story*-

Two weeks after I found out I was pregnant with our oldest daughter, the school year ended and I didn't return to teaching, so I had a lot of time to sit around and daydream and imagine what life with a baby would look like. In my pregnancy journal, I scribbled down my hopes and I confided my fears. Chief amongst my worries and concerns about this newest chapter in our life was the impact a baby would have on our marriage.

Kyle and I had celebrated our sixth wedding anniversary a month after I became pregnant with Dacey. We had a lot of marriage, a lot of shared history, a lot of routine and "normal" behind us already. Or so it seemed at the time. I absolutely adored my husband, and I loved the happy little life we had built. Saturday mornings and doughnuts in bed with the newspapers, frequenting the theater multiple times a month to catch the latest releases, long talks on long road trips, and staying up way past bed time, each of us quiet and lost in books.

At times the thought of all that changing would almost paralyze me.

Even within church culture, I heard a lot of messages about the precariousness of marriage in the child-raising years, and how critical it is to be hyper-sensitive to meeting the spouse's needs before the children's. What I read from Christian authors writing on parenting seemed to further validate my concerns; scenes of overwrought, emotionally drained and unavailable spouses were painted in vivid colors, and I knew that was what I desperately wanted to avoid. And so instead of thinking proactively about honoring our marriage after we became parents, I was mostly playing mental defense, subconsciously setting up our unborn child as an adversary, someone whose very presence was sure to wreak havoc in our marriage.

-Laura's Story-

Mark and I had been married for nearly seven years once Maya was born, and were very accustomed and attached to our life as a two-person household. While we were certain that we wanted to have children, and thrilled to discover we were expecting, there were definitely moments of "*what* did we just do?" woven into the joyful anticipation.

I carried the same weight of fear and trepidation that Megan did over what might become of my marriage when the baby arrived. And many of those fears were based upon things I had read or heard from others. It always seemed to me a confusing experience to be fielding congratulations, squeals of glee, and blissful sighs of, "oh what a precious gift from the Lord!" and then at the same time come across so many stern warnings about not letting our precious gift from the Lord believe that they are *too* precious, lest they try to take over our home and ruin our marriage. Um ... what?

Like Megan, I felt almost as if I was to steel myself against my baby's intrusion if I was to truly honor my marriage. Love and nurture this little one, but make certain that she grows up knowing that Daddy comes first. These messages, when considered by a very hormonal first-time mother desperate to please God, maintain her good-wife status, and parent her baby perfectly, became a recipe for some seriously high anxiety levels.

And then the most wonderful thing happened in each of our homes. We became parents. And it changed our marriages.

Calling Out the False Dichotomy

As we reflect back on our own fears about the negative ways that parenting can affect a marriage, we've discovered a core issue: **somewhere along the way, a false dichotomy has been created, one that says you must either give precedence to your spouse, *or* to your children.** This dichotomy creates a view on family life in black and white terms, when the reality is that life with children often ends up lived out in the gray areas.

Operating under this false dichotomy very naturally leads to fears about what life with a new baby will do to the marriage relationship. It's easy to see how we were both prone to fearful imaginations of life with a baby wrecking our marriages. How could we possibly maintain our performances as loving wives when our days were going to be spent caring for the baby? As a new parent or parent-to-be, it only makes sense to take on a defensive stance, mentally and physically holding baby at arm's length in order to minimize intrusion and discomfort in the marriage.

Throughout the Bible, it is clear that God takes the matter of marriage seriously. In the New Testament, the Apostle Paul often uses marriage as an illustration for how Christ loves the Church and for how we, the Church, ought to response to His love. Not only is marital strife and discord harmful for the two people who are bound together through marriage, it's also damaging to the witness our lives should be as people whose hearts and lives have been changed by Christ's love. Our covenants to each other and God in marriage aren't just for us. They allow us to be signposts to a watching world about what life in Christ can look like. Clearly, nurturing a healthy marriage is incredibly important.

When new parents buy into this false dichotomy, thinking that the couple must choose to give priority to the spouse *or* the children, they may find themselves pressured into creating circumstances to prove to each other and to others that the spouse takes precedence. For example, one book we read suggested that baby be placed in a swing or bouncy seat for fifteen minutes every evening while mom and dad sit on the couch to talk. This was to be done in full view of the baby so that baby could see and understand that mom and dad were secure in their marriage to one another. In this advice, we see evidence of that false dichotomy again, forcing a separation between parents and child, making a point to create physical space between them.

At the end of a long day, it may very well be that mom is happy to find a reason and space to disconnect from baby for a little while, and we would never speak against that very real need. But let's pause and consider a few aspects of "couch time."[18]

First of all, are babies really capable of understanding that their parents are building relationship as they sit on the couch together? And secondly, what if evenings are a precious, all-too-brief time for working parents to reconnect with baby after a day away from them? Kyle always loved the attention he received from his daughters when he came home from work — even when they were babies — and Megan was happy to hand off a little one for a few moments of rest.   While we certainly don't condemn practices such as "couch time," we question how helpful they actually are in modeling to our children a strong, Christ-centered marriage.

---

18   The term "couch time" was coined by Gary Ezzo in his book *On Becoming Babywise*.

Another way we've seen this emphasis on spouse over children is through a subtle insistence on practicing date night. Date nights are fun, wonderful and often much-needed in order to continue to connect with each other on an intimate level. We wholeheartedly agree with that! What we've run into in our own lives and have heard from other parents, however, is that when the new baby arrives, there is often pressure on parents to leave the baby with a grandparent or babysitter as soon as possible, as a way to build a defensive front by going out alone.

Not everyone feels comfortable with leaving babies that early, and for breastfeeding mothers whose babies won't take a bottle, it can be nearly impossible. One or both parents may feel guilty for leaving baby, but then also feel guilty for not leaving baby. For confessed homebodies like Megan and Kyle, an evening at home together with a movie and take-out after the babies were in bed was much more enjoyable and in some ways offered more of a chance to reconnect than if they had forced themselves into a date night when neither of them felt comfortable with it.

We realize that much of this advice to carve out time with your spouse is rooted in good principles. It is important to be intentional about marriage, no matter what season of life you find yourself in! What we would like to do, however, is advocate for a view on marriage and parenthood that is holistic rather than adversarial. Freedom to embrace the principle of marriage-building, while seeking how that is best lived out in your unique relationship. We are discovering in our own lives that parenting under the leadership of the Holy Spirit has been the source of much growth and contributed to unity in our marriages as we have drawn closer together and to God.

Creating a New Paradigm

Becoming a parent doesn't happen without some shock to all of our systems. In fact, there is research to support the fact that it can be quite traumatic: a study published in 2009 by researchers from Texas A&M University and the University of Denver found that 90% of 218 couples showed marital strain and deterioration in some form following the birth of the couple's first baby.

We have to wonder, however, what would happen if we embraced a new paradigm? **What if we tossed out the false dichotomy of our culture that insists that you must choose to be a good spouse *or* a good parent, and chose instead to embrace a model of marriage that emphasized unity, growth, and partnership?** What if the upheaval and uncertainty parenting brings could be redeemed into an undeniable opportunity to grow closer to Christ and closer to one another?

One of the most beautiful aspects of a healthy marriage is the way it is always evolving, shifting to meet the needs of both spouses, allowing them to move forward with clasped hands and interwoven hearts. The months of parenting an infant together are ripe with opportunity to grow even closer to the person you have pledged your love and life to through the covenant of marriage. Within a new paradigm for marriage, we see three specific areas where growth can occur: service, communication, and partnership.

Embracing Growth through Serving

In his book *Sacred Marriage*, author Gary Thomas examines the idea that perhaps God uses marriage to make us holy, rather than happy. Chapter by chapter, he encourages couples to allow themselves to be changed—not by their spouses, but by Christ himself. One particularly challenging chapter is titled, "Make Me a Servant:

Marriage Can Build in Us a Servant's Heart." Throughout the chapter, Thomas reminds us

"to be a Christian is to be a self-volunteering servant."[19]

He speaks to the fact that marriage with the intent of servanthood in mind runs completely contradictory to our cultural expectations, to say nothing of its opposition to human nature in general.

Included in the chapter is a selection from Gary and Betsy Ricucci's book, *Love that Lasts* in which they observe that the homemaker tending to the laundry and washing a sinkful of dirty dishes may wonder about the significance of her work. They remind us that,

"in God's eyes, nothing is more significant than servanthood. The path to genuine greatness lies in serving."[20]

Throughout this chapter on surrendering to the idea of serving one another, Thomas looks at how marriage confronts us in our selfishness and affords us the chance to become more like Christ in our choice to serve our spouses. He writes,

"To fully sanctify the marriage relationship, we must live it together as Jesus lived his life – embracing the discipline of sacrifice and service as a daily practice. In the same way that Jesus gave his body for us, we are to lay down our energy, our bodies, and our lives for others."[21]

These are challenging, convicting words, yet undeniable in the accurate picture of service modeled by Christ.

19   Gary Thomas, *Sacred Marriage: What if God Designed Marriage to Make Us Holy More Than to Make Us Happy?* (Grand Rapids, Michigan: Zondervan, 2000), 180.

20   Thomas, *Sacred Marriage*, 182

21   Thomas, *Sacred Marriage*, 187

Both of us have mused that before we had children, it was actually fairly easy to serve our husbands. Yes, we each had jobs to tend to outside of our homes, but beyond that and a few family obligations, nothing else tugged at our time. In short, it was easy to serve because we didn't have much else to do. The true meaning of sacrifice in the context of service didn't become real to us until after we became parents and had *unceasing* demands on our time, thoughts, and energy.

What we've noticed, however, is that parenting from inside a framework of gently meeting the needs of our babies has allowed us to be keenly aware of our spouses' needs as well. In choosing to follow the promptings of the Holy Spirit as we mother our children, it is imperative to call on Christ and ask Him to empower us in our daily tasks. As He fills us with his Spirit, we not only become sensitive to the needs of our children, we also become sensitive to the needs of our spouses.

There is perhaps no greater moment in time in the life of a young family for husbands and wives to serve each other in love than in that first year of parenting. For us, this has looked like Kyle rubbing Megan's feet at the end of a long day of holding and swaying with Dacey in arms. When she was four months old he sent Megan off for a ninety-minute massage. Heaven! And his ability to prepare an evening meal rescued her from late afternoon stress on many occasions.

Mark's unfailing support and presence during nighttime feedings ministered deeply to Laura's heart. The way he jumped in to change diapers, picked up the slack on laundry and dishwasher-loading duties, was a second pair of hands to help with a slippery, wet baby at bath time, and took the morning parenting shift on the weekends so Laura could sleep in, made it so clear to her that the two of them were a team.

As wives, we've listened in the moment to hear our husbands express a need and sought ways to support them. Sometimes it meant getting up a little early to iron a shirt for work or staying up a little late to finish a movie he wanted to watch. Sometimes it meant engaging in the financial conversation that we didn't feel much like having because we knew that getting those things in order would bring him peace of mind. And sometimes it meant simply remembering to genuinely kiss him hello when he walked in the door from work.

Choosing to serve another when you are well-rested and have your wits about you is noble. Choosing the path of servanthood when you are sleep-deprived and suffering from Mommy or Daddy Brain is miraculous. We cannot truly serve anyone without seeking the power of the Spirit. When we feel we have nothing left with which to serve our spouses, we can turn to Scripture for encouragement and prayer for empowerment.

For example, Romans 5:5 reminds us, *"God has poured out his love into our hearts by the Holy Spirit whom he has given us."* And we might pray something like, *"Father God, please fill my heart with your love, a love that is not selfish or self-seeking, but a love that esteems and serves others. Please fill me with your Spirit that I might serve you by serving my husband today."*

Within this new paradigm of marriage, our lives have been enriched in boundless ways as we have surrendered to following Christ on the path of servanthood.

Cultivating Growth through Communication

Anyone who has ever written anything on marriage *ever* has emphasized the importance of communicating with your spouse, so this idea is nothing new. But there are unique seasons of life where intentionally practicing good communication is pivotal for the overall health of the relationship. Caring for an infant forces us to rely on good, healthy, and helpful communication with our spouses, not only to survive, but to thrive within those intense days together as a family.

Parenting under the leadership of the Spirit can be emotionally and physically exhausting. And when we are tired, there is always the temptation to withdraw into isolation or to suffer in silence, yet the yield for these choices is nearly always bitterness, resentment, and anger. But when we face the end of ourselves, we discover the beginning of God's power working within us.

When faced with the very real challenges of caring for little ones, each partner has the opportunity to open up to the other about the burden he or she is carrying or an area where support is needed. This is when communication with each other must be specific. Wives: don't assume your husband will just know when you need an hour or two out of the house alone—communicate it clearly. Husbands: don't insist that your wife should be able to sense that you are feeling like an outsider—help her to understand your perspective.

It's important to keep in mind, too, that for some personalities and temperaments, this heightened need for authentic communication can be challenging. Some may not feel comfortable with showing sincere vulnerability. One or both partners may be fully invested in the self-reliant mask they've created through the years, and the thought of revealing themselves as anything less than fully competent can be terrifying.

In the midst of intense moments, practice speaking and listening with transparency. A healthy marriage is one in which there is no shame in revealing weakness. When we create a safe place with our spouses to lower our I've-got-it-all-together masks, there will be an opening of fresh and powerful channels of communication that we might never have dared to explore before our children were born.

Just as parenting can reveal a need to communicate during the rough spots, it also affords the chance to share unspeakable, exquisite joy with another. In the earliest days, take time to sit together and marvel at the magnificence of the baby you have created together. As new milestones are reached and time turns that wee baby into an adventurous toddler, make space to soak up the wonder of it all.

For Laura, I'll admit that before we had children, Mark and I only ever used our dining room table when we had guests over for a meal. The two of us would eat dinner nearly every night on the couch in front of the television. After Maya was born and began eating some solid food, we sort of grudgingly decided that if family mealtime was going to be an important thing in our home in the years to come, we might as well start now.

For the first few nights, it was almost awkward, the three of us sitting there together during dinner. Soon, though, we were surprised to find how much we began to value that focused family time. I heard more about Mark's work experiences than I used to, and found myself opening up more about the high and low points of my days at home. We talked to Maya, laughed about her new antics and began conversations that carried into the rest of the evening hours. What began as a way to lay a nurturing foundation for our children carried into our marriage as well, as it gave us another regular opportunity to build communication—even with our little one's participation.

The days spent parenting a baby can feel so long at the time, but it's such a short season in the grand scheme of life. Communicating the joys of the day is a powerful way to minister to one another and encourage each other to focus on gratitude and thankfulness, even (and especially) when it's been a bad day.

Encouraging Growth through Partnership

Because of the all-day, every day nature of parenting, there is tremendous opportunity to work together in partnership during these years. One thing we've learned over and over since our first children were born is that there are few things in life that allow us to learn to trust each other more deeply and draw on each other's strengths more willingly than parenting.

For Megan, about three months before our wedding, we had the chance to do a ropes course together with a Sunday School class. Kyle, a born athlete who exudes confidence in all physical activities, was completely at ease with the idea of slipping along ropes hung high in the air, tethered to the ground by a mere rope with me at the other end. I, on the other hand, was terrified. I knew I had neither the physical strength nor the mental toughness required to get through the course.

Kyle zipped along the ropes more quickly than anyone and seemed to actually enjoy himself. When it was my turn, my shaking hands could barely grip the lines. I was woozy and scared and the wind was relentlessly whipping around me, threatening to blow me off course. Yet from the ground, Kyle never ceased to call up encouragement and praise to me. Two steps into the course, I wanted to quit, but Kyle urged me on, insisting that I was stronger than I thought and that I was safe. Finishing that ropes course was exhilarating beyond just the sense of accomplishment; it cemented for me that Kyle was really, truly a partner I could count on, even and especially in my weakest moments.

Those earliest months of motherhood were very much like being up on that ropes course. I had never done anything like it, and I was completely unprepared for how hard it would be. I was shaky and unsure, distraught by the smallest misstep. Yet Kyle showed up again as my anchor on the ground: encouraging, praising, and believing that I was going to make it through.

From the beginning when God created man and woman in His image, He had in mind that we would live in communion with one another. The new paradigm we'd like to see in marriage is one that isn't on the defense against the interruption of parenting, but rather embraces the positive changes parenting brings to marriage. In fact, by partnering together in parenting, marriages are made stronger as together husband and wife seek God for the best direction for their family.

Living Out a New Model of Marriage

Sometimes we need the extra dose of courage and boldness that comes with knowing we aren't the only ones resisting the false dichotomy of marriage and parenting that permeates our culture. We have heard from many parents who are carving out ways to follow this new paradigm in marriage, one that embraces the change that parenting brings and seeks to engage that change in positive ways within marriage.

Here are some insights others have shared with us as they have reflected on parenting and marriage:

> God has shown us so much in parenting. My husband has come to know Christ through parenting, and I have come to know the Holy Spirit more deeply. We have prayed together, cried together and loved much deeper than ever before. We cherish moments of sexual connection, date nights, quick kisses in passing. We used to take those moments for granted, but now we treasure them as blessings. We give each other more grace as we extend grace to our children. After six years of being parents, our marriage is stronger than ever before. God has blessed

us with these girls, and we lean on each other through the tough moments. It's not all peachy, sometimes we bicker and complain about how the other disciplines or cares for the kids, but then we show forgiveness and grace to each other and our girls get to see that love is more than roses, it is a commitment with God. – Steph, Iowa

In the beginning, being a mother wasn't blissful like all my other books said it should be. It was almost torture. Owen had colic and screamed like a crazy man from 2 p.m. to 11 p.m. Daily. Until he was four months old. Through all of this, we surprisingly grew closer. Sean would show me how he swaddled Owen and why that calmed him down. I'd tell Sean which songs seemed to work to put Owen to sleep. And finally, after Owen was asleep in between the two of us, we'd bond over episodes of CSI, our reward for parenting this incredibly high-needs child. It's still working. Sean is patient and doesn't get frazzled like I do. He knows how to be the opposite parent of what I am, and I think that makes us work so great together: our parenting styles complement each other in a way I could have never imagined. – Erin, Nevada

After seven years of parenting together, we've learned that we are a team and we need to trust each other to remain unified. My husband so appreciates that ever since the kids were babies I never left him lists of what he had to do, or schedules, or how to do things while I was out. Even though he did things differently, he did them with his own kind of Dad Love. And, sometimes it even turned out better than I would have told him to do it. That was big for me as a control-loving person. – Amy, New York

*Once we had children, our marriage took on an entirely
new role. Our marriage was a wonderful relationship
before children; after children it has become an institution.
An institution built on a relationship but now fortified
with steel girders of support and responsibility. There
are many times when dealing with our children results
in us "neglecting" our personal relationship. But we are
strengthening our union by working for a common goal
with little thought for ourselves. Our marriage is bigger
and more important than we are now. It is our family's
little fortress. – Cathy, Kentucky*

Navigating the "new normal" of marriage after children arrive is
not easy. It requires a level of selflessness previously unknown,
and can bring a variety of growing pains. It need not, however, be
a source of fear.

It is not necessary to train your baby to understand that your
marriage is a top priority in the home. Your children will grow
up recognizing that fact as they watch you live life alongside
one another, modeling a servant's heart, unconditional love,
unwavering support in your relationship, and a joint commitment
to the Lord. And while parenthood will undoubtedly change your
relationship with your spouse, we want to offer the hope that as
you work hard at understanding each other, serving one another,
and committing your marriage to prayer, this change can be one
that ultimately brings you closer together and closer to God. You
can be sure that He will gently and unfailingly respond by pouring
His Spirit into your lives and your marriage, as the perfect Father
that He is.

There is no reason that nurturing a marriage and following the
Spirit's promptings to meet our children's needs must be mutually
exclusive. We can each testify with certainty that we have never

felt as much peace, joy, or fulfillment in our homes or our hearts as we have in the times where we've embraced both of these aspects of family life. And we are both profoundly thankful to God for allowing us the glimpses of His very nature that are revealed in the moments when we walk in true servanthood towards our husbands and the little loves we've created with them.

Chapter Seven

As We Keep the Spark

Sex after kids. It's a very real concern on the minds of new mothers. And (let's be honest) it's definitely on the minds of new fathers! *Can it ever be the same again?* What about the extra time and attention that the baby requires, particularly for parents who find themselves prayerfully led away from a more systematic approach?

Fear over the fate of a couple's sex life is a common hurdle we have experienced in ourselves and in others when it comes to embracing the freedom to follow the Spirit's lead in parenting. As we discussed in the previous chapter, the numerous warnings against approaching baby-care in *any way other* than certain prescribed regimens tend to focus heavily on the marriage relationship as a potential casualty of stepping outside the box—and intimacy, according to these sources, is usually the first thing to go.

Is this true? Will straying from one particular set of parenting methods inevitably turn you from lovers to strangers? In this chapter, we will offer our own experiences and those of others as an answer to these questions, and offer some tips on how to keep the sparks flying as you parent together.

-Laura's Story-

It was one of those nights when a romantic mood had hit both of us at the same time. The sun had set, the house was quiet, and we headed for the bedroom, smiling in anticipation. If this were a questionable reality television program, the camera would have swung suddenly to the closing of a door with a "Do Not Disturb" sign flung hastily over the knob. Lights dim as the picture fades...

This evening would not remain the picture of an idyllic love scene for long, however. The lights in our room came immediately back on as the cries of a hungry three-month-old rang out suddenly — and loudly — from across the hall. Not exactly mood-enhancing. After a few frozen seconds of wishful "maybe it's a fluke and she'll go back to sleep" thinking, we accepted the reality that this rendezvous would need to be placed on hold. Irritated, I trudged to Maya's room to change and feed her, and Mark went out to flip through the channels on the living room television.

As I sat in the rocking chair, mind switched back to "mother" position, complaints and grumblings took over. Well, here's another major life change! For seven years now we've always been able to take advantage of this time of day to concentrate on each other. We have a great thing going here. Or ... we did.

Behind the griping were some budding seeds of guilt. Unfortunately, this wasn't the first time we had been interrupted during attempts at intimacy. And I was beginning to feel as though it were my fault. Although my confidence in stepping away from mainstream parenting methods was growing stronger each day, I still remembered the promises and warnings contained in the pages of the books I had read during my pregnancy.

One of the most rattling pictures presented had been one of a crumbling sex life, where there was no longer time or energy for lovemaking, and husband and wife began to live as romance-deprived roommates. And while I hadn't seen glaring signs of such calamities in my marriage as of yet, evenings like this stirred up the nagging fear that perhaps they were just around the corner. If I would just give in to feeding schedules and sleep training, would we have fewer interruptions? Was that more important? And ... oh, no ... are we going to turn into one of those sex-less couples from TV sitcoms?

-Megan's Story-

The six week appointment. You know the one. It's the visit where your doctor or midwife checks you out, makes sure everything post-birth is healing properly and then clears you for exercise.

And ... oh yeah ... sex.

I was dreading it. For six weeks, I had spun a cozy cocoon of new motherhood around myself. The baby who was so fresh from my own body still shared in my body for most of the day and much of the night. I spent most of the day nursing her, changing her diapers, washing bitty baby clothes, obsessing over her sleep problems, and bouncing her through her evening crankies. It was hard work and it was exhausting, but I was spending that babymoon time the way everyone expects you to spend it — totally wrapped up in my baby.

But after the six-week appointment, it's like BAM. There's a new expectation there, one that is more honeymoon than babymoon, and yeah — I was dreading it. I was barely getting this new mama thing down, and now I felt like I had to switch gears totally and get my wifely groove back. I already felt like I was failing at motherhood during that time. What if it turned out I was going to fail at meeting my husband's needs, too?

So the six week appointment came and everything checked out. Hooray! Hooray? Our return to sex was far more awkward than it was awesome. We found ourselves in the guest bedroom because Dacey was asleep in our bed. For the first time, we had to be mindful of not being too loud. My ears strained for sounds of her stirring and I was completely distracted by worry of what would happen if she woke up. *Nothing* was the way it had been before, and I began to wonder if the years of having a great sex life were destined to become a distant memory as parenthood took over every aspect of our lives.

What Really Happens to Intimacy when Baby Comes Home?

We've all heard the tales of marriages where the romance fizzled as parenthood began. Does the parenting style you embrace really make or break your sex life? Let's take a look at some of the common fears and perceptions on this subject, as well as some suggestions for how to keep this aspect of marriage very much alive and well — even with an infant in the house!

To begin with, God intended for us to delight in every aspect of our marriages, and sex should be a gift we cultivate, explore, have fun with, and pray over. (Yes, pray over! More on that later.) In the newlywed days, of course, tending to this part of the relationship is second nature. Most couples find, though, that the fire can flicker a little bit over time, as stresses pile up and familiarity causes flirtation to wane. There are seasons in every marriage that require a conscious choice by both spouses to give intimacy a kick-start.

It is particularly important to be deliberate about keeping the flame stoked as we move into parenthood. Free time is suddenly gone, everyone is tired, and life is full of new responsibilities and less-than-racy conversations. *"Which diapers worked best for the blow-out* *poop again?" "Do I even **have** any shirts without spit-up stains?"* There is no doubt that extra care must be taken to nurture the romantic relationship after adding children to the family, as circumstances inevitably make quality time together more challenging.

Too often, however, Christian parenting manuals seem to approach the subject of sex after baby in a way that focuses on fears while offering a particular infant-care methodology to protect a couple's love life. Some popular elements of these viewpoints tend to be:

- An implication that a less-scheduled parenting philosophy could lead to complete disarray in the intimacy between husband and wife.

- The idea that without the free nights resulting from a sleep-trained baby, husband and wife do not have the proper time for intimacy.

- The fear that allowing baby in mom and dad's sleeping space for any amount of time compromises the intimacy of the marriage bed. (We address this further in Chapter Nine.)

These are perceptions we once held, and outcomes we once feared. And while we understand the cautions behind these points, we now respectfully yet confidently disagree with the ultimate conclusions. As each of us was drawn by the Holy Spirit to the parenting path He had for us, we found that our sex lives with our husbands changed. We faced interruptions at inopportune times, had to work around nighttime feedings and seasons spent sharing our bed part-time with little ones. Our pre-established routines were thrown out the window.

And can we tell you a secret? Things eventually got better than ever before. Seriously!

No doubt there were a few rough spots in the beginning. Maybe more than a few. But just as in the previous chapter we spoke of how parenting together by the Spirit's leading has strengthened our marriages, we have found that the growth in those relationships has caused our intimate lives with our spouses to find new levels of depth and excitement.

As awkward as it can feel[22] to bring up this topic for discussion, we truly believe that there should be more opportunities for safe, appropriate discussions about sex—especially in Christian circles, where the subject is often considered taboo. And if we are going to offer encouragement to parents in following the Lord's lead and not getting wrapped up in unnecessary fears, this whole sex thing is so important to address. It's a big deal. So we're going there. (Sorry, Grandma.)

Four Sources for Enjoying Sex during Parenthood

There are a few specific things we have found to be absolute lifesavers as we've seen this area of our marriages adjust to the realities of parenthood.

Communication

"Let's talk about sex, baby." Although we are endorsing neither Salt nor Pepa, this is one thing that they did get right. We need to talk about sex! So much squeamishness about sexuality exists within our Christian sub-culture that even the God-given gift of marital intimacy begins to feel hush-hush and secretive. This makes it

---

22   This seems like a good place to break in with the admission that it is more than a little strange to be writing about our sex lives in a book that will have our names on the cover and that people who know and love us will be reading. Like our *grandmothers*! And friends we'll run into *at church* and *the grocery store*! (Commencing hyperventilation.)

difficult, particularly for those who grew up in a home where sex was one of those *things of which we do not speak*, to achieve a healthy comfort level in discussing the matter. Within a marriage, though, it is imperative that this aspect of the relationship is one where there is open communication, especially when you are adjusting to life as parents.

For the first six weeks after baby's birth, intercourse is technically off-limits. But jumping right back into the swing of things after the all-clear at your doctor's visit isn't always as easy as it would appear. For some women, there is significant physical discomfort to deal with, depending on the specifics of the birth process. For others, the mental hurdles are more difficult. Nursing a baby all day long does not necessarily inspire a great deal of excitement about sharing your body with yet another person, and the shift from *source of food* to *object of desire* takes some time to sort out. A lot of us also have a difficult time accepting our bodies in the post-partum stage, and while every talk show discussion featuring new fathers seems to indicate with great certainty that they don't care in the slightest and still find us beautiful and desirable, our internal dialogue often sounds like, *"That's all well and good, but I don't even recognize myself right now."*

Women need to learn to work through this concern with communication. If we don't speak it, our husbands can only guess at what we are feeling.

For Laura, I've struggled with life-long hang-ups about my appearance anyway. After giving birth, I couldn't even stand to glance at myself in the mirror. I wanted to be intimate with Mark — I really did. I just couldn't get past the thought of him looking at me in my post-partum state, and didn't quite trust his assurances. I mean, he *has* to say that stuff, right?

What finally broke through for me was a moment when I found myself mumbling an actual apology to Mark for my body. The look on his face was one of such genuine bewilderment, and so clearly communicated the question, "Are you a *crazy* person?" that it finally clicked for me that he really didn't see the problems that I did. He truly did find me desirable. And it was so sweetly funny that the tension I was feeling began to ease. I was able to share with him how I was feeling about myself, he was able to tell me what he saw when he looked at me, and I finally started to believe him.

On the flip side, it's easy for wives to forget how deeply rooted the need for sex is in our husbands. In all of our exhaustive caretaking of the newest member of the household, even the most supportive and understanding of men can begin to feel slighted when their advances are met with sighs of resignation instead of enthusiasm.

For Megan, I had always prided myself on being an enthusiastic partner in our dynamic duo of intimacy. I never resorted to headache excuses, and I initiated encounters at least as often as Kyle did. The physical and mental toll of new motherhood brought that pride tumbling down, and for the first time, I found myself gently rejecting Kyle's advances. The chill in the air between us woke me up to the fact that we needed a repair in the rift between us. As much as it made me squirm, I knew we were going to have to dig in and talk through this issue together.

With all of the previously mentioned fatigue and disorienting new responsibilities, the need to communicate more deliberately about all facets of life rises dramatically in parenthood. It's just that some subjects are a little easier to bring up than others, right? "Honey, I just realized that we're both overdue for dentist appointments." *Normal.* "Oh hey, I have a sexual need that's gone unfulfilled in recent months." *So not normal.*

It should be. Ideally, there's really no reason that a conversation with your spouse about sex should be any more awkward than discussing where to have dinner on Friday night. What's working? What's not? Is anything getting in the way of your connection with each other? If you are able to speak openly and often about physical intimacy together, these conversations can give you a crucial understanding of each other's needs in this new season of life.

If a conversation of this nature isn't a familiar one to either of you, it might be helpful to approach it slowly. Maybe schedule a conversation a few days away. Take some time to think individually about the points you'd like to get across and what you are really asking for. Then you can each come into the discussion a little more prepared and clear-headed. You're likely not going to resolve every aspect of your intimate relationship in one conversation, but testing the waters of communication is almost certain to be a step in the right direction.

Does talking face-to-face about sex just really seem too uncomfortable? Perhaps you could start by communicating in notes back and forth. Jot down a few thoughts or suggestions and slip them into a shared notebook. Wives, your husband may not love the idea of writing out his thoughts, but a reminder that this could re-charge a lagging sex life might just inspire him to pick up a pen!

Whatever communication style best suits your personalities and comfort levels, we would encourage you to push past the awkwardness that you may feel at first, open up a few discussions about sex, and see what happens.

When we broached this subject on Megan's blog, several other mothers chimed in about the importance of talking through intimacy issues:

Communication, specifically regarding the bedroom, is really hard for me. I've never been able to talk about sex very openly, and I feel all vulnerable. But I find it's so rewarding when I do, because my gosh, he LISTENS to me! (And gets all excited as well!) - Misty, Tennessee

Communication about likes and dislikes has helped to make sex more enjoyable. We've been working on this part of our marriage for two years and through four kids, and I can honestly say that I now ask for it as often as he does! The more you look to serve his interests, the more he will generally reciprocate, and your marriage as a whole will only get stronger. – Sara, Virginia

Flexibility

Of *attitude*, friends. Flexibility of *attitude*.

In the time before children enter the picture, visions of perfectly romantic moments and long, uninterrupted times behind the bedroom door can keep your expectations at idealistic levels. With a baby in the house, however, there are just bound to be bumps in the road. You will be interrupted at inopportune times by an early awakening from a nap, an unexpected request for a nighttime feeding, or an ill-timed diaper explosion. (Mood-killer, anyone?) You will encounter situations where a much-anticipated intimate encounter must be postponed slightly due to a flare-up of evening fussiness.

The best thing to do when this sort of distraction threatens to derail a romantic plan? *Just roll with it.* Is that the easiest response? Not a chance. Especially for new moms, as we sometimes have a difficult time making the mental switch from mother to lover anyway.

What each of us has found is that when we can keep a flexible attitude about our intimate moments with our husbands, we begin to enjoy them more ... dare we say even more than before we had children? When we let go of the pressure to achieve a pre-planned, perfect experience, we find opportunities for memorably unique encounters that can be pretty perfect in themselves.

For Laura, maintaining an easy-going attitude in the midst of interruptions was very difficult at first. But I've also learned that it really comes down to choices in those challenging moments. I can choose to get all huffy and frustrated when the unexpected happens, working myself right out of the mood and into a pouty state of mind, deciding that it's pointless to try to enjoy any romantic time with my husband until we can leave the baby with a babysitter overnight in two (or ten) years. Or I can choose to take a deep breath and chuckle about it together, allowing the expectation of continuing our rendezvous (whether it be minutes away or a few hours) to become a fun part of the experience. I've gained the delightful discovery that flirtatious anticipation is way more fun than irritated defeat. *Way* more fun!

This change toward increased patience and flexibility has carried over to other aspects of my life and relationships as well, and is yet another gift I've received from stepping outside the parenting box and allowing God to refine me.

Creativity

You probably already know this, but we're going to reveal it as if it were a secret revelation of genius. *There is no rule that says that sex must happen after dark ... or in your bed.* The whole "not tonight, dear" punch line of cartoon strips and television shows, where mom and dad fall exhausted into bed and are faced with the do-we-or-don't-we question can give that impression. But if we're all being honest, isn't the very end of the day often the very *last* time we really feel like putting any energy into an intimate moment? At that point it can be difficult to stay awake long enough to mumble "goodnight." Considering other times we might slip in some romance can help fight the fatigue factor, as well as spice up a hum-drum routine.

Perhaps early evening could be an ideal time to concentrate on each other, when you can get the baby to sleep and then make your date time the focal point. Then cuddle up on the couch afterwards with a bowl of ice cream. Putting sex at the top of your evening free-time schedule means that you are giving your best attention to each other first. Or what about taking advantage of the daylight hours? A spontaneous afternoon encounter can be both exciting and rejuvenating, as can an, "Oh hello, here we both are behind closed doors getting dressed for the morning ... hmmm ..."

In the new-baby stage, creativity is crucial. The time periods between feedings and diaper changes can be brief and sporadic. Take advantage of those precious few moments when the little one falls asleep in the swing, or find another cozy nook of the house in the days when the bassinet occupies your bedroom. During a co-sleeping phase of life, why not create a challenge to see how many different spots in your home can be turned into the scene of romantic trysts? Thinking outside the box is a good thing, and the excitement and spontaneity could even make you feel like flirtatious newlyweds again! (For real!)

> *We've found "afternoon delight" to be just as fun, and a good way to get out of a rut as well. All too often we just go about our business, not seeing each other, let alone touching, during that crucial naptime. To stop blogging, folding laundry, or watching TV can feel annoying in the minute, but once we're done it's like being newlyweds again! – Misty, Tennessee*

We've had to get creative when it comes to the realities of life with young children. I would say our favorite coping technique is to steal any available moment. DO NOT WAIT. So many times, I've winked at him and said, "Later!" only to fall asleep the moment my sweet little cheek hit the pillow. So now I force myself to put aside the To Do List and the day-to-day concerns and seize the moment when it presents itself. – Kelly, Minnesota

Prayer

We know. It seems ... weird. And more than a little awkward. As we've said several times already, though, there is truly nothing outside the scope of the Lord's wisdom and guidance and nothing that we can not take before Him in prayer. The God who brought you together and made you one flesh desires that your marriage thrive and flourish in every respect.

If praying together with your spouse over issues of intimacy is just too uncomfortable, perhaps start with confessing your own areas of struggle. Wives, are you finding yourself putting sex on the To Do list as just one more thing to check off? Could your husband be picking up on the less-than-appealing fact that your participation is often nothing more than simply fulfilling your wifely duties? Ask God to do a deep work in those heart-attitude issues and to fill you with a deep longing and enthusiasm for physical intimacy with your husband. Pray that He would remove any self-conscious thoughts about your post-baby body and help you to accept—even delight in— your husband's desire for you. You may be surprised at the difference it can make!

Husbands, are you having trouble with cultivating a sensitive and supportive attitude toward your wife as she balances her roles as wife and mother? Have you sought to truly find out what she needs from you as her partner so that you can serve her in Christ-like love and romance her in a way that makes her feel beautiful and desired? Pray that God would open your heart to understand your wife intimately at an emotional level. There is perhaps no bigger turn-on for her.

> *It sounds strange, but I cannot emphasize enough the difference inviting God into the bedroom has made in our intimate life. When I prayed for the Spirit to change my heart, to remove the resentment, my jealousy of what I saw as "MY" time in the evenings, and to give it all to Him, it was like falling in love with my husband all over again.* — Karen, Iowa

While all four of these elements are helpful ones no matter which parenting style you follow, they are particularly helpful if you've chosen to adopt a Spirit-led mindset as you care for your baby. Creativity is essential if you are led to a season of co-sleeping, for instance. Flexibility is a lifesaver when dealing with night-waking or nap-waking struggles that make for more frequent interruptions. Communication covers it all, making certain that the connection is solid and circumventing possible misunderstandings or needs (of any kind) going unmet. And prayer is, quite simply, the lifeline that binds us together, with Him at the center.

Final Thoughts on Fanning the Flame

Friends, there is no question that new parenthood is flat-out exhausting. Sleepless nights take their toll on your energy level, and there always seems to be a load of laundry to fold or neglected dishes in the sink. There are plenty of times when the last thing you feel like doing is giving your body or your baby-free time to someone else. But if we can ask ourselves questions like, *"When do I feel most energized?" "Am I giving my spouse any of that time?" "What do I need in order to feel connected emotionally or physically?"* and then talk with each other about those things, we're not only serving our spouses—we are giving ourselves the gift of a sex life that can be lively instead of draining, fresh instead of mundane, and "let's enjoy each other" instead of "let's get it over with."

A healthy sex life carries over into other areas in the marriage as well. Petty disagreements over diaper duty are far less important when you're still glowing from that shared shower during the baby's afternoon nap. Anticipating some alone time later in the day leaves you both less likely to gravitate separately toward your phones and e-mail and more likely to spend free moments in smiling, wink-filled conversation. During a time when life can seem stressful and topsy-turvy, continuing to fan the flame of your romantic relationship serves as an important reminder of the fun and familiar.

While having a baby will most likely change a couple's sexual relationship in some ways, there is no reason for it to suffer. You won't feel fired-up in the bedroom all the time—you just won't. But there are most definitely steps you can take to nurture the intimacy. And while those popular infant-rearing philosophies suggest that certain parenting methods can invite doom into your sex life, we simply disagree!

Both of us have found that despite our initial hang-ups, the extra attention and effort we've given in order to keep our intimate relationships with our husbands on track have served to bring them to a point of deeper health and vitality than at any other point in our marriages, even while the Spirit prompted us to care for our babies in ways that require more time and connection at all hours. Preserving a vibrant sex life is not dependent upon the parenting methods you decide to follow, but rather on the mindset you keep.

It means choosing, no matter the season of life, to make romance a priority. It takes time, it takes adjustment, and it takes commitment. We are here to tell you, though – it is … *wink* … worth it!

Chapter Eight

As We Encourage the Connection

Uh-uh-uh! Better put that baby down! You'll spoil her!

Oh, it's good for babies to cry. It helps their lungs to grow!

We're humans, not kangaroos! No need for us to stick our babies in pouches.

Oh, the joys of parenting. From the moment a baby bump is detectable to the day your baby packs up to leave for college, everyone has advice for you. Some of the most-often repeated words of advice for new parents centers on the idea of not spoiling the baby.

Both of us heard plenty of this advice when we were new mothers. Yet this conventional wisdom caused an extraordinary amount of conflict. Nobody wants to be the parent of a spoiled child, but we both found we had the overwhelming desire to cuddle our babies far more often than what was advised. In the earliest months of parenting, we lived in tension between wanting to engage with our babies in the moments they were awake and feeling nervous about giving them *too* much attention.

-Megan's Story-

For the first few months of Dacey's life, I tried so hard to follow a parent-directed schedule during the day. I so badly wanted her to sleep through the nights, and I was just sure mistakes in our daytime routines were to blame for her nighttime wake-ups. I was tired, desperate, and determined to follow the advice of a parenting book to the letter.

One afternoon when she was about two months old, she had awakened from a nap cheerful and alert. I nursed her and then laid her in the playpen for her to have independent play during her wake-time, just as the book advised me I should do as part of our daily schedule.

This was just after she had started smiling on a regular basis, and I can still see that gummy, toothless smile as she looked up at me from the playpen. I felt a pang as I walked away, conflicted over wanting to just sit and play and snuggle with my daughter, but feeling quite sure that doing so was squashing her chances at learning independence, and worst of all, teaching her to be clingy and demanding because of all of the attention I was giving her.

I thought of all of the off-hand comments I had heard directed at babies who cried when left in bouncy seats or infant swings: "Now there's a baby that gets held too much!" and "Well, somebody is spoiled rotten, isn't she?" No, that wasn't going to be my baby. I decided to ignore the urge to pick her up and play and left her lying in the playpen watching her mobile spin. This was better for her, wasn't it?

-Laura's Story-

From the first day of motherhood, I claimed naptime as my time to rest and relax. And I discovered by accident during a period

of time in Maya's babyhood that she would nap better and longer if I happened to be holding her as she slept. The comfort of my presence, warmth of my body, and rhythm of my breathing seemed to make for more complete naps and happier wake-ups. So ... get this ... for a period of a few months I cuddled her on the couch almost every day during naptime, while I read, watched television, or dozed.

This definitely fell in the unacceptable category in terms of the advice I'd read and received. But I loved every single minute of it! The sense of bonding, the way it forced me to take time out to rest and rejuvenate, the bittersweet knowledge that this was likely to only be a first-child experience. Too soon, that season ended and it worked better to have her nap in her crib again—a transition which was quick and seamless. I still look back and treasure those peaceful afternoons.

By the time this was happening, I knew full well that I was parenting outside the box and that this little piece of information about our naptime habits would not be received well by most people. In fact, after letting it slip to a couple of friends and family members, I had to endure regular nervous-sounding, frozen-smiled questions. "So, are you still ... um ... letting her nap...on you?"

There was genuine, best-intentioned concern there for me, I know. And I'd like to say that by that point I was completely confident in tuning out critical voices and listening to God's alone. But even as I was parenting with more assurance and looked forward each day to our snuggly naptimes, the questions and comments still caused me to wonder whether I was sliding hopelessly off-course. All it takes are a few seeds of doubt before the same fears start sprouting up all over again. *Am I going to regret this someday?*

A Push For Early Independence

Though we have moved fully into the twenty-first century, much of our culture's attitudes toward parenting are still saturated with influence from the twentieth century. Parents are allowed to *ooooh* and *ahhhh* over a newborn, but a few weeks later the reminders of last century's no-nonsense approach to babies come to call with warnings about spoiling a baby by holding it too much or creating little monsters by attending to baby's cries.

One man in particular had an extraordinary influence over parental practices in the early twentieth century: Dr. John Broadus Watson. In his book *Psychological Care of Infant and Child*, he expounds on the happiness to be found in being "self-reliant, productive, and void of emotion."[23] As culture in the United States began to reflect the values of capitalism and the expansion of industry, independence became an increasingly sought-after character trait to cultivate in children.

During this time, there was a movement to maintain careful distance between yourself and your children. Dr. Watson wrote:

> *Treat them as though they were young adults. Dress them, bathe them with care and circumspection. Let your behavior always be objective and kindly firm. Never hug and kiss them, never let them sit on your lap. If you must, kiss them once on the forehead when they say good night. Shake hands with them in the morning. Give them a pat on the head if they have made an extraordinarily good job on a difficult task. Try it out. In a week's time you will find how easy it is to be perfectly objective with your child and at the same time kindly. You will be utterly ashamed*

23   Suzanne Houk, "'Psychological Care of Infant and Child" A Reflection of its Author and his Times [Internet – WWW, URL] http://www.mathcs.duq.edu/~packer/DevPsych/Houk2000.html, 15 March, 2000

of the mawkish, sentimental way you have been handling
it.[24]

Of course, this may all seem downright laughable to us, but it's important to understand this was the advice given to our great-grandparents. Some of Dr. Watson's views eventually fell out of favor, and by the time our grandparents were raising our own parents, Dr. Benjamin Spock was making waves with his view on parenting that encouraged parents to trust their instincts.

Dr. Watson would have a hard time finding a publisher for his advice today, but there is no denying the residual effect of the directives he and his peers gave to parents of that era and the influence this maintains in Western culture. You don't have to look far to find parenting books that promote independence and self-reliance for babies long before such an expectation would be developmentally realistic.

The fact is, there is a reason babies cry and there is a reason parents instinctually respond to those cries: God created babies to be dependent on us! And within the miracle of His perfect design for each human being, He created within all of us a need for connection.

The Need for Connection

When we think about humanity being created in the image of God, it makes sense that the triune God — the three Persons of the Trinity — would create people who, from birth, need connection with others. The Father, Son, and Holy Spirit are inextricably connected. In our physical beings, there is nothing we as people can compare that sort of connection to, but there is most certainly an intrinsic need for others hard-wired into each person created by God.

24   Ibid

That tiny newborn snuggled up in receiving blankets is utterly helpless and completely dependent on others meeting his physical needs of food, shelter, hygiene, and safety. But beyond these physical needs, he has an intense need for interaction. Much research has concluded that it is this interaction with others that stimulates baby's brain to continue to develop after birth. As part of His miraculous design for mankind, God ensured that at birth, healthy newborns have developed just enough to be able to *survive* – but if a newborn is to *thrive* after birth, it will only be because of connection to a care giver:

> *The human brain takes time to develop, so nature has insured that the neural circuits responsible for the most vital bodily functions – breathing, heartbeat, circulation, sleeping, sucking, and swallowing – are up and running by the time a baby emerges from the protective womb. The rest of brain development can follow at a more leisurely pace, maximizing the opportunity for a baby's experience and environment to shape his emerging mind.*[25]

Thoughtful, attentive connection to a baby not only meets his needs in infancy, it also sets him up for a greater capacity to learn as he gets older:

> *Recent research on early brain development has established that babies are born with virtually all their neurons already formed. However, the connections between these neurons are in large part established and elaborated after birth. This occurs due to the massive sprouting of extensions from neurons, called dendrites, which become receiving points for dendrites from other*

25   Zero To Three, "FAQs on the Brain" [Internet – WWW, URL] http://www.zerotothree.org/child-development/brain-development/faqs-on-the-brain.html

neurons. This process creates synapses which forms the "wiring" of the brain, and allows various areas of the brain to communicate and to transmit information that ultimately allows coordinated functioning.

The human brain is genetically programmed to produce more synapses than it will ultimately need. By eight months of life a baby may have an astounding 1,000 trillion synapses in his or her brain. By the late preschool years there may be about twice as many connections that eventually will be preserved into adulthood.

Researchers found that when mothers frequently spoke to their infants, their children learned almost 300 more words by age two than other two year olds whose mothers rarely spoke to them.

Other studies showed that the mere exposure to language such as listening to TV or to adults talking among themselves provides little benefit. They concluded that infants need to interact directly with other human beings — to hear people talking about what they are experiencing and seeing — in order for them to develop optimal language skills. Evidence also indicates that infants and young children who are denied meaningful language input and interaction may fail to develop neural connections and pathways that are necessary to facilitate later learning. [26]

Far beyond *goo goo gah gah,* babies need to hear their parents talking to them, narrating the day as it unfolds around them, telling stories rooted in the real and the fantastical, and engaging with them in

---

26   The University of Arizona Medical Center, "Babies' Brain Development and Human Interaction" [Internet – WWW, URL] http://www.umcarizona.org/ body.cfm?id=964

a way that values them as fellow human beings. In the words of the wise Dr. Seuss: *because after all, a person's a person, no matter how small!*[27]

The Source of Connection

The fact that babies are born with an intense need to connect in order to stimulate brain development and social awareness is only one part of the healthy baby equation. Just as God instills in infants this need to connect, He also equips parents to have the desire to meet that need.

The National Center for Infants, Toddlers, and Families states it this way:

> *Infants prefer human stimuli — your face, voice, touch, and even smell — over everything else. They innately orient to people's faces and would rather listen to a speech or singing than any other kind of sound.*
> *Most adults (and children) find infants irresistible, and instinctively want to nurture and protect them. It is **certainly no accident that the affection most parents feel towards their babies and the kind of attention we most want to shower them with — touching, holding, comforting, rocking, singing and talking to — provide precisely the best kind of stimulation for their growing brains.** Because brain development is so heavily dependent on early experience, most babies will receive the right kind of nurturing from their*

---

27   Dr. Seuss, *Horton Hears a Who* (New York: Random House, 1954)

earliest days, through our loving urges and parenting instincts.[28]*(emphasis ours)*

Just as God created in babies a need for connection to allow their developmental needs to be met, He also created in us a parental instinct that is driven to meet those very needs. A baby born to indifferent adults would be significantly less likely to experience healthy brain development. And so there is a reason that parents find *their* babies to be so consuming, even people who do not get warm fuzzy feelings for other babies: it is part of God's grand design for the healthy growth and nurturing that is pivotal throughout the months of infancy.

The benefits of interaction with a baby are not limited to healthy brain development; it also lays the foundation for a child's ability to process and express emotion. Consider this insight from author Lauren Lindsey Porter writing for *Mothering* on "The Science of Attachment."

> *Babies, who are not born with the ability to decode and decipher meanings and emotions, rely on the mother to help them navigate the world, both internal and external. This relationship allows for the formation of 'internal working models' that function as scripts by which babies can then gauge their own emotions and those of others.* [29]

Though this particular article places emphasis on the mother-child relationship, we believe that within a co-parenting dynamic, a

28   ZERO TO THREE, "FAQs on the Brain" [Internet-WWW, URL] http://www.zerotothree.org/child-development/brain-development/faqs-on-the-brain.html

29   Lauren Lindsey Porter, "The Science of Attachment," Mothering July-August 2003

baby benefits from this connection to *both* parents as they learn to organize the dizzying array of stimuli that they encounter each day. As we've said before, during the first year of life, babies seem needy because, well, **babies are needy!** They are utterly dependent on caregivers to care for all of their daily needs. And until they grow into toddlerhood, crying is the only way they have to communicate those needs. The conventional wisdom that insists that you'll spoil a baby by holding her too much or responding to her cries is in direct conflict with God's design for the way parents interact with babies.

One parenting book we read suggests:

> *Experience teaches us that parents who desire to demonstrate true love to their children will put aside their own emotions for the sake of the child. They will tolerate a little crying if, by their assessment, doing so is the best plan of action for the baby — such as when baby needs to settle in for a nap or a restful night's sleep.*[30]

While this seems logical on the surface, what we detect in the author's encouragement to "put aside their own emotions" is, in all reality, a suggestion that parents ignore the emotional response that God instills in us to prompt us to meet the needs of our littlest ones. Further, it seems to us that true love is most powerfully displayed not in the toleration of crying, but rather in the sacrificial giving of ourselves to those who are incapable of verbally expressing wants, needs, or even gratitude.

This is not to say that you can *always* attend to *every* cry. If you have other children, the baby may have to cry for a while as you attend to the needs of siblings. Meals need to be prepared, phone

---

30   Gary Ezzo, On Becoming Babywise (Sisters, OR: Multnomah Books, 1995)
      127

calls should be answered, and bills must be paid. Additionally, some babies are colicky or suffer from severe digestion issues and cry for many hours each day regardless of whether or not a parent is available to soothe them. There is no doubt that baby will have to be left to cry for a few moments as a matter of practicality, but these moments are generally exceptions for parents who embrace the importance of connection during baby's first year.

The Practice of Connection

Intentional connection with baby doesn't mean you spend 100% of baby's awake time playing with him on a play mat on the floor. Connection is more of a frame of mind and a way of life than it is a set of rules or must-dos. There are, however, some practices that can make connection with baby during the first year a little more practical for parents in day-to-day life.

Babywearing

Though it seems like a recent trend made popular by sling-wearing celebrities, babywearing is a practice that dates back to ancient civilizations. Centuries before playpens, baby monitors, and infant car seats, babies had to be a lot more portable. A mother couldn't leave her helpless little one in a tent or hut as she went about the business of the day, so she would simply use cloth and common sense to fasten her baby to herself as she worked. Wherever mom went, baby went, too.

Though it is no longer a matter of baby's survival in our culture, there are still many benefits to both baby and parent in the practice of babywearing.

Practicality: When parents are committed to responsive, instinctive, and connected parenting, some practical issues do arise. Carrying a baby in arms can be physically exhausting. A baby carrier of some kind (sling, wrap, or soft-structured carrier) takes the pressure off of a parent's arms, back, and shoulders while allowing baby to still be physically close and connected to the parent. Parents are also allowed to be more hands-free to attend to other things while baby is secure in a carrier. Megan found babywearing to be incredibly helpful with Aliza Joy, who could take naps in the mei tai carrier she used while Dacey continued in her normal routine of park visits and play dates.

Protection: Babies can be so irresistible to others. Grandmotherly -types at the grocery store want to reach out and stroke baby's cheek and preschoolers at church want to touch baby's soft hair. Babies worn in carriers are instantly protected from exposure to all manner of well-meaning but unwanted touches.

Proximity: Babywearing enhances baby's learning through proximity to the parent who is wearing him. Dr. William Sears explains:

> *It's easier to understand babywearing when you think of a baby's gestation as lasting eighteen months – nine months inside the womb and at least nine more months outside. The womb environment automatically regulates baby's systems. Birth temporarily disrupts this organization. The more quickly, however, baby gets outside help with organizing these systems, the more easily he adapts to the puzzle of life outside the womb.*
>
> *By extending the womb experience, the babywearing mother (and father) provides an external regulating system that balances the irregular and disorganized tendencies of the baby. Picture how these regulating systems work. Mother's rhythmic walk, for example (which baby has been feeling for nine months), reminds baby of the womb experience. This familiar rhythm,*

imprinted on baby's mind in the womb, now reappears in the 'outside womb' and calms baby. As baby places her ear against her mother's chest, mother's heartbeat, beautifully regular and familiar, reminds baby of the sounds of the womb. As another biological regulator, baby senses mother's rhythmic breathing while worn tummy-to-tummy, chest-to-chest. Simply stated, regular parental rhythms have a balancing effect on the infant's irregular rhythms. Babywearing reminds the baby of and continues the motion and balance he enjoyed in the womb. [23]

Proximity to parents encourages an "organized" baby. Organized babies are generally happier babies who are able to spend more time learning and less time processing life outside the womb.

Peace: Generally, though not always, babies who are worn tend to be less fussy. Again, Dr. Sears sheds some light on this:

In 1986, a team of pediatricians in Montreal reported on a study of ninety-nine mother-infant pairs. The first group of parents were provided with a baby carrier and assigned to carry their babies for at least three extra hours a day. They were encouraged to carry their infants throughout the day, regardless of the state of the infant, not just in response to crying or fussing. In the control, or noncarried group, parents were not given any specific instructions about carrying. After six weeks, the infants who received supplemental carrying cried and fussed 43 percent less than the noncarried group. [31]

There are a multitude of reasons why a baby might be fussy, ranging from acid reflux to sensory processing issues to general temperament, and babywearing is certainly not the cure-all. It

31   Ibid

might be worth a try, however, to help both baby and parents find a few moments of peace in the midst of a cranky day.

Because of the recent surge in the popularity of babywearing, there are plenty of options when it comes to choosing a carrier. Reading message boards devoted to babywearing might be a good place to start, as would a local La Leche League chapter or a brick-and-mortar natural parenting store.

Once you adapt to a babywearing lifestyle, you may be surprised to find like-minded parents are excited to share their own babywearing stories with you. Here are a few that other parents have shared with us:

> *My first baby is now 40 years old, and we practiced baby wearing before it was even a term. I improvised a sling from a beach towel, and carried him all the time. He was a fussy baby who seldom slept more than fifteen minutes, day or night. Carrying him did not solve our problems, but gave me the constant assurance that he was okay, even if he was crying.*
>
> *It makes me laugh when new mothers tell about "discovering" baby wearing, as if it is something new. It goes back to the beginning – mothers have known instinctively that always being in touch with the baby is kind of like always being in touch with God. Challenging, stretching, often uncomfortable, but ultimately nourishing our bonds with each other. – Jan, Texas*

> *I have practiced babywearing with both of my children (ages three and four months), and there is nothing like wrapping them up in the sling, cinching it close, and having that beautiful little head right under my nose. My baby falls asleep almost instantly and we snuggle through our errands. The smell of my baby is intoxicating. Having*

him that close reminds me to stop and pay attention to him in the midst of errands, chores around the house, or whatever else I might be doing. It reminds me that my children's needs are more important than checking things off of my list. Though he is much too big to wear now, I believe the foundation of babywearing has gone a long ways towards giving my three year old security and confidence and me a loving and supportive attitude towards parenting. – Jodi, Florida

While babywearing works beautifully for some parents, it is not for everyone. There are parents who don't enjoy it or can't do it for physical reasons, and there are certainly babies who don't like to be worn, too. Far from creating a mandate for this practice, we simply offer it as one way to encourage connection with your baby.

Baby in Family Life

Parents can easily spend hundreds and hundreds of dollars on blinky, noisy gadgets on the market today that are meant to enhance baby's enjoyment of life. Babies learn just fine (and perhaps derive more enjoyment) from being included in the rhythms of daily life.

As a baby grows through the first year of life, she will very naturally want to be where the action is. Look for ways to bring her into what you are doing. Though they are little and don't verbally express themselves, they still long for interaction with those they love, just as grown-ups do. As Kittie Frantz, a highly-respected breastfeeding advocate and pediatric nurse has famously said: "Remember, you're not managing an inconvenience, you're raising a human being."[32] A pivotal aspect of connected parenting is respecting baby on a person-to-person level.

---

32   Kittie Frantz, Geddes Productions home page [Internet-WWW, URL]
      http://www.geddesproduction.com/

When the Connection is Broken

We've spent time talking about the God-given instincts that compel us to respond to the needs of our infants and older babies, but there is another aspect of connection that we want to address: the effects of postpartum depression. When PPD is a reality in the life of a new mother, it can seem impossible to practice connected parenting.

What is PPD?

We are obviously not medical experts. In fact, neither of us has personally experienced PPD. We felt it was extremely important, though, to highlight the reality of this difficult journey faced by so many new mothers, and we are honored that friends who have walked the road of PPD have offered their insights for us to rely on as we move through this section.

We have found the simplest definition of PPD to be depression, anxiety, or compulsive thoughts and behaviors that begin in the month following the birth of a baby. The majority of women experience "baby blues," or feelings of instability and hormonal upset in the weeks following birth. As Katherine Stone of Postpartum Progress writes:

> We all have bad days. Postpartum depression and anxiety are not just bad days. Women with postpartum depression or anxiety have symptoms like these most of the time, for a period of at least two weeks or longer, and these symptoms interfere with their ability to function as they would like on a daily basis.[33]

---

33   Katherine Stone, "The Symptoms of Postpartum Depression and Anxiety (in Plain Mama English)," [Internet-WWW, URL] http://postpartumprogress. com/the-symptoms-of-postpartum-depression-anxiety-in-plain-mama-english

Postpartum depression is a complicated, complex disease, and as Katherine said, its symptoms make it impossible for a woman to function normally, let alone establish and build a connection to her baby. A mother battling PPD must pursue her own health and healing before she is able to make an effort to pursue connection with her child.

Stories of PPD

In order to provide an authentic look at how PPD can affect mothers, we wanted to share the words of some moms who have experienced it first-hand. You can find lots of information and published literature on the topic, but sometimes beyond clinical definitions and sterile medical discussions, the stories of others are able to provide the most powerful insights.

Postpartum depression manifests itself in ways that vary from woman to woman. Some of these mothers have boldly and courageously shared with us what PPD looked like for them:

> *On the fourth day postpartum, I started crying. I just felt overwhelmed in a way I had never experienced before. I didn't want to do the newborn thing. I wanted to hide in bed all day. I would nurse the baby as needed, but then I wanted my husband to take her in the other room. I honestly felt like her joining us was a really bad thing for our family. As I thought about the next year of sleepless nights and teething, and other normal baby things, I couldn't bear it, and I wanted to run away from home.*
>
> *It really took me by surprise, because on some level I felt like I was stronger or better than that — like it should be a mind over matter thing whether or not I feel depressed. I would pray daily that my days would be brighter, and that I would be happy to have her. One day I sniffed*

at the baby's head and thought that I really didn't like the way she smelled. That's what changed everything for me. My biology background reminded me that my newborn should be highly attractive to me. The fact that she smelled bad made me realize that something was biologically WRONG! I knew I was sick and that I needed help because hoping for the best cannot fix the chemical/ hormone imbalance that must be occurring to make her unappealing to my senses.

At five weeks I saw my midwife and admitted I had a problem. She first made sure I didn't want to hurt the baby. "No," I responded, "I just want her to go away." Then my wonderful midwife gave me a hug and told me that this was okay. She told me that I'm not a bad mama, and that I just needed a little help. I was so thankful for her reassurance that sometimes PPD happens, and it is normal, and there are people trained to help us move past (and medications if needed). She referred me to a therapist who specializes in PPD. This was the start of my recovery. – Victoria, Los Angeles

Cerys was a very much wanted baby for both myself and my husband — we were overjoyed when I got pregnant and my pregnancy was very easy. She eventually arrived fourteen days overdue by emergency caesarean section after a 40 hour induced labour, which was spent flat on my back hooked up to every possible monitor. At the time I was too exhausted to pay much attention to the quiet voice that whispered "failure" every time I tried to process what had happened.

Colic kicked in at six weeks. Cerys would only sleep for 45 minutes at a time and need feeding and up to an hour of pacing and rocking to get her to sleep. "You'll still be doing this when she's five," the voice shouted at me every time it was my turn to get her to sleep, as my tears fells silently.

Then one night I lost it. Nothing was getting Cerys to sleep and I just couldn't take it anymore. I shoved her into the arms of my husband and went downstairs. I sat on the floor paralyzed with despair. I cried so hard I couldn't even talk. I knew this had to stop. I was ruining everyone else's lives as well as my own. After a couple of hours I decided that something had to change. I needed to go. It was for everyone's benefit. I was just becoming a burden. Cerys was better off without me, and if I went now, my husband would surely find someone else who could take better care of him and Cerys.

I wanted to die – to end it all permanently. I could see no other way – how could I come back from all these failures I had stacked up in just a few weeks? But I knew there was only one way that I could do it – my job in a mental health team had taught me that. I wanted to get a room in motel – one that would be far enough away to ensure that my husband, Cerys or other family would never have to go near it afterwards.

Then morning came. My husband and my parents supported me in getting the help I desperately needed.

It took until Cerys was about a year old before I could say that I was mostly 'better,' and by better I mean that my stomach would not clench up in fear at the thought of having to look after her for a whole day while my husband went to work. I want to be able to write that God instantly healed me. But it was a much slower process than that, and I still have low periods now from time to time.

Although my husband, immediate family and a couple of very trusted friends knew what was going on, I felt very ashamed of my depression and certainly never shared it with anyone at church, although I imagine some of them may have guessed. Although I was desperately clinging to God throughout, I could not bear the thought of any more people thinking I was a failure, particularly as a mother and a Christian. For a long time I could not pray to God in words, only in tears, but now I can see that this was important as at least I was being real with God about what was going on, rather than pretending all was well. It has made my relationship with God much more authentic.
– Nicola, UK

Coming to terms with the reality of PPD can be difficult for many women. As these women have noted, it is common to feel like a failure as a spouse, a mother, and — in some faith communities — as a Christian.

We wanted to share stories from women who are followers of Christ who have battled through postpartum depression, each of them crying out to God for direction and wisdom on how to find healing from it. For some it will involve intense sessions with a mental health professional, for others it might be counseling and medication to boost the body's ability to find its way back to equilibrium. The most important thing we want to emphasize is that it is pivotal to seek help, and it is imperative to seek guidance from the Spirit of God in how to pursue healing.

Our friend Stephanie, a mother of three in West Virginia, shared with us briefly about her battle with PPD and how she has found redemption through the healing that followed:

We came home with our first baby, and I was a miserable, hormonal mess. I remember resenting her intrusion into

*our content, peaceful marriage — and she was a "planned"
baby! I prayed constantly that the Lord would take these
feelings away from me — and thinking that the reason
I was having problems was because I wasn't praying
enough. Oh, how I convinced myself of that.*

*I would drive to the grocery store (alone) and pray that
someone would hit me and kill me so I wouldn't have to
go back home. That sounds so heartless now, but I truly
felt like I was in a hopeless situation. I cried every day
that I wanted it to go back to the way it was before. Thank
God I had an incredibly patient, understanding husband
who encouraged me to get help, and so many friends that
I could lean on and be transparent with.*

*I began seeing a Christian counselor and started taking
anti-depressant medication. As the months passed, I
regained some normalcy and we got pregnant again but
my OB and I were so concerned about another round
with PPD that I kept taking the anti-depressant. I didn't
experience any PPD after my son and it was truly a night
and day experience. It's been a learning experience, for
sure. I am so thankful to share this story so other women
can know there is no magic formula, no strict chart that
makes you the perfect mom — it's all about letting God be
the guide! I can't tell you how I wish I had known that
seven years ago, but I promise you it's what I go by now.*

In our resources section, we'll share more information on where to
go to find hope and healing from postpartum depression. If you are
finding it difficult or painful to pursue connection with your baby,
it may be that seeking some outside help can help you know if there
is a bigger issue at play.

Deepening the Connection to God

When both mother and baby are healthy and able to engage in connecting with each other during the season of infancy, there is much more than healthy brain development and social awareness happening. To the parent tuned in to our Heavenly Father, there is a fresh revelation of God's overwhelming love for His children.

Something wondrous and mystical happens in our hearts and minds when we become parents. **For the first time, we gain a glimpse of what God must feel for us, His children.** We begin to understand that we are all made of the stuff of His heart, and that we have the capacity to reveal His heart to those around us. We are best able to radiate His love when we are most connected to Him.

Once we had the courage to reject conventional wisdom that minimized the importance of connecting to our babies and to fully embrace a mind-set that found joy and fulfillment in nurturing that bond, we discovered a new sense of awe and wonder in our relationships with God.

With newly tendered hearts, the passages of Scripture that speak of God's love for us came to life in Technicolor:

"See what great love the Father has lavished on us, that we should be called children of God! And that is what we are!" - I John 3:1 (NIV 1984)

"No, in all these things we are more than conquerors through him who loved us. For I am sure that neither death nor life, nor angels nor rulers, nor things present nor things to come, nor powers, nor height nor depth, nor anything else in all creation, will be able to separate us from the love of God in Christ Jesus our Lord." – Romans 8:37-39 (ESV)

"I have loved you with an everlasting love; I have drawn you with unfailing kindness.". – Jeremiah 31:3 (NIV)

There are moments in parenting our children when we feel as though our hearts might burst, so deep and extravagant is our love for them. How incredibly and wonderfully kind of God to allow us to experience this level of connection to our children that we might know a little more of how He loves us.

Parenting a newborn helped me develop a particular insight into my relationship with God. In the early days of my son's life, I remember holding him close, enjoying the warmth, cherishing those involuntary sleep-smiles; but, oh, I longed for him to reciprocate my affection. Of course, I continued to care for him as best I could, but when I finally saw his first real smile and felt his first hug (I melted with each little pat on my back), it was thrilling. I wonder if this might be how it is with God. His love for us is never failing, but he also longs for his children to turn our attention to him in worship. I've been challenged to be more aware of my expression of love and gratitude toward God. And though my attempts pale in comparison to the love I have received, perhaps they are like the hugs of an infant, sweet delight. – Megan, Kentucky

I think being a mom has dramatically changed my sense of connection to God. In the same way visiting an historical site brings new meaning to the stuff you learned in a high school class years ago, parenting my own child has infused my relationship with my creator with new life. As I reflect on my own love for my daughter, I have daily epiphanies about his nature. I know you don't have to be a parent to have this understanding. Some people find it in nature, in their work or in other relationships. But for me, being a mother has been as much of a vehicle for bringing me closer to him as it has to my daughter. – Jennifer, Virginia

For some, it is through the process of parenting children that they are able to find redemption and healing from their own troubled childhoods. In experiencing connection within a healthy and functional dynamic, they discover a new understanding of God's plan for families as a safe place of love and growth:

My relationship with my mother growing up was difficult. When I found out I was pregnant with a baby girl something cemented in my heart for her, and for all my children — that they would never, ever question my love for them. I just adore pouring out affection and affirmation on my little girl. Ironically through this my relationship with my mum has become closer. As she has watched me love my own kids, she has realized and admitted that she had some shortcomings when we were growing up — most of which stemmed from her feelings that she should have been doing things the way her mother did them. It has been healing for me watching her and my dad interact with my kids, and to see how much they adore them and how fantastic they are with them. And I think it's allowing all of us to show a bit more emotion and support than we used to. – Sarah, New Zealand

In God our Father, each of us has the perfect parent. He never turns from us, no matter how needy we may be. He refuses to leave us in puddles of tears and angst, but instead sends His Spirit to comfort us. He sits with us through the lonely night and quenches our deepest needs. He even spoke through the prophet Zephaniah that He rejoices over us with singing.[34]

It is through the lens of parenting that we can grasp the shocking truth of God's unrelenting pursuit of connection with us — that He

---

34   Zephaniah 3:17

would send His own Son as atonement for the sin that separates us from Him.

> *Parenting affected my connection with God almost instantly. I remember so clearly rocking Noah as a newborn in his nursery and the realization flooding from my head to my toes — how in the world would I ever be able to sacrifice my only son like God did for me? Boggled my mind. I was overwhelmed with this for days, and honestly even still, these almost 11 years later."* – Stephanie, Indiana

Such an unfathomable sacrifice on the part of a Father who couldn't bear to be disconnected and separated from His beloved children because of their sin. It should be no surprise that a God who loves us so intensely would create us to desire that bond with our own children. To ignore the emotions that compel us to meet the needs of our infants would be to ignore part of what makes us image bearers of Him.

Oh, how we wish we could visit the new mother versions of ourselves. We would giggle over the "spoiled baby" warnings and whisper of God's perfect design for baby's best start in life. We would offer assurance that there is nothing indulgent or unhealthy about hearing a baby's cry as communication, nor can you spoil a baby rotten by attending to her needs.

Megan would tell herself to pick Dacey up out of that playpen for a snuggle no matter how often she felt the urge. Laura would reassure herself that she would most definitely never regret those precious naptimes spent with Maya. We would say, with tears in eyes, that independence from mom and dad will come soon enough, and that all too soon these needy little babies will wriggle down and run confidently into the life that awaits them beyond the reach of our arms.

Chapter Nine

As They Sleep ... Where?

Can you keep a secret? This is a big one, so we're really hoping we can trust you here.

We sleep with our babies.

Now, depending on the culture of the region in which you live, right now you are either wondering, *"Why on earth would co-sleeping be a secret?"* or you are looking around to make sure no one is reading over your shoulder a book filled with shocking admissions like these. Interestingly, opinions on co-sleeping with babies vary widely and are largely determined by what cultural norms have been set and are followed by the people in the community.

In pockets of western culture that are deemed more "crunchy" or prone to natural family living as well as in most Majority World cultures, co-sleeping with children is an accepted norm. However, in much of western society, sharing sleep with babies is a taboo topic, one that is discussed in whispered confessions and only with trusted friends.

In fact, it was a topic talked about so little in our circles (and in such disparaging tones when it was discussed) that both of us were determined to avoid the practice altogether. No one was more surprised than we were to discover that co-sleeping saved our sanity during our earliest months of mothering.

-Megan's Story-

Before Dacey was born, I knew I didn't know much about parenting, but one thing I did know for sure was that our baby would *not* be in bed with us. We got a bassinette so the baby could be near us at night, but the experts in all the books warned us that babies belong in their cribs from the beginning, and allowing a baby in bed with the parents only sets everyone up for heartache down the road.

Obeying this crib mandate was so much easier when it was all theoretical principle rather than actual reality. As I lay in the hospital bed in the early hours of Dacey's first full day of life, I studied her features with deliberate intensity, mesmerized by the rise and fall of her chest with each miraculous breath, silently worshipping God for His amazing creation. I found myself inexplicably compelled to have her right next to me, right there in the bed, even though I knew I shouldn't. Finally, the burgeoning power of maternal instinct overwhelmed my allegiance to prescriptive parenting advice, and I tenderly scooped her up and nestled her next to me.

Each time a nurse came to check on us, I cringed, just sure someone was going to ask why Dacey wasn't in the bassinette, just knowing someone would call me on breaking the rules. No one, not one of those postpartum care nurses, said one word to me about the baby sleeping next to me in bed. Still, I couldn't help feeling guilty.

You can imagine, then, how much the guilt piled up when we got home with our beautiful, almost 10-pound baby and I discovered that because she was such a hefty newborn and because I was recovering from a C-section, I could only nurse her lying down which meant that she often fell asleep with me. In our bed. Our *marriage bed.*

-Laura's Story-

It all started when Maya was about nine months old. It had been a particularly interrupted night, and as she finished up a feeding in the early morning hours I could hardly fathom the thought of getting up once again to walk back to her crib. So ... I didn't. In a move driven by pure fatigue, I simply placed her gently beside me, snuggled up close, and fell into a blissful sleep. Incredibly, we all slept well past her usual (far too early) wake-up time! I can't even describe the joy of that extra rest. We had stumbled upon a way to soak up some additional sleep. And as an added bonus, it was such a lovely feeling for the three of us to wake up together. Pure delight!

I had never really considered co-sleeping before that point, although I wasn't completely certain as to why. Based upon things I had heard, the subject was just somehow filed in my brain under the category of "not a good idea." As the nights went on, though, we found ourselves turning this new discovery into a routine. After the last feeding of the night (or sometimes even after the first one) Maya would join us until morning. It worked out splendidly!

And yet, I felt strangely guilty. As if I were encouraging something inadvisable, shameful, wrong. I had heard people speak in unequivocal terms about not allowing children into the "marriage bed." So although we were all happy with our new sleeping arrangements, and while I had never felt closer to my husband, I struggled for quite some time with feeling as though we were somehow inviting doom by breaking the rule of a child-free bed. I couldn't quite let down my guard as I waited for that other shoe to drop. Even now, as I've more than come to terms with the idea of part-time co-sleeping and its place in our home, I still feel as though I'm making a confession when I say that we sometimes sleep with our babies.

It seems that I find the most resistance to the subject among those in my Christian circles. My admission of our seasons of co-sleeping, or my suggestions of the same to friends who are battling sleep issues with their own babies, are often met with wide eyes, a brisk shake of the head, and an insistence that, "I could never do that. No." And these comments are likely to be followed by a mumbled reference to the marriage bed or "my place with my husband."

Co-sleeping explained

Co-sleeping is an umbrella term under which all kinds of sharing sleep space practices fall. Dr. James McKenna, the foremost researcher on the topic, defines co-sleep as "the broad practice of sharing the same sleep environment."[35] Sometimes this means bed-sharing, other times it means baby sleeps within arms' reach of a care giver, and still other times it could mean room-sharing where baby sleeps in a bassinette, crib or on some other sleep surface in the same room as care givers.

Sharing a sleep space is a practice as old as humanity itself. Long before cribs were mass-produced and insisted upon by every baby magazine's "Must Have for Baby!" lists, parents have shared sleep spaces with their children. There is even a biblical mention of the practice in the text of Luke 11:7 where Jesus conveyed the annoyance of a man interrupted by a friend at midnight saying:

"Do not bother me; the door is now shut, and my children are with me in bed. I cannot get up and give you anything."(ESV)

Long before 2000-square-foot homes in which every family member had his own bedroom and his own bed, the cultural norm was sharing sleep.

---

35   Dr. James McKenna, *Sudden Infant Death Syndrome: New Trends in the Nineties.* (Oslo: Scandinavian University Press, 1995) 256-265

So what changed? In the era of western culture that gave rise to people moving away from agricultural life and into more urban settings, the matter of where a child slept at night became a status symbol of sorts. Families who were wealthy enough to have separate bedrooms for children probably did so, along with purchasing cribs and small beds in which the little ones would sleep.

In the early twentieth century, views on family changed drastically as modernization of everything from childbirth to feeding infants became heavily influenced by popular science of the era. Practices that had long been biological and cultural norms such as breastfeeding and bed-sharing gave way to new norms for family life. James McKenna and Thomas McDade note:

> The popularity of scheduled bottle feeding in the 1950s only reinforced the idea that uninterrupted solitary crib sleeping was "normal." In the late 1950s and early 1960s when electro-physiological technology became more available, breastfeeding was at an all-time low in the USA, with fewer than 9% of mothers leaving hospitals breastfeeding. Both cow's milk and/or formula were encouraged by medical personnel and thought to be superior to human milk. Hence, pioneering sleep researchers had no reason to question the appropriateness of quantifying "normal" infant sleep (sleep architecture) and arousal patterns under solitary sleeping conditions using bottle fed infants with little or no parental contact or nighttime feedings.[36]

So for several generations throughout the twentieth century, co-sleeping was rarely practiced in western culture. The opinions,

36   James McKenna and Thomas McDade, *Why babies should never sleep alone: a review of the co-sleeping controversy in relation to SIDS, bed sharing and breastfeeding.* Pediatric Respiratory Reviews (2005) 6, 134-152

beliefs, and practices of our grandparents and parents can't help but shape our own beliefs on these issues, and a residual hesitance to practice co-sleeping is still evident in our culture.

If sharing sleep with an infant is a biological norm that has been practiced by people for many centuries, what are some of the reasons it is still actively avoided by many westerners? Some obvious reasons include fear, medical issues, practical issues, and comfort.

Fear: Because of the widespread prevalence of anti-co-sleeping messages found everywhere from crib packaging to brochures in pediatrician's offices, many people are simply afraid to sleep with their babies. New parents are given many precise directives on how to make crib sleep safe for a baby, but there are very few resources that empower parents to practice safe co-sleeping, so parents may be fearful of rolling over on baby or of baby falling out of bed. A second kind of fear when it comes to co-sleeping is the fear that it will cause problems in marriage, a topic which we'll discuss more in depth momentarily.

Medical issues: For babies who suffer from acid reflux, a semi-upright position is far more comfortable then sleeping flat on any kind of sleep surface. Additionally, parents may have their own medical issues such as sleep apnea or a need to take sleep medication that prevents them from sharing a sleep space with a baby.

Practical issues: Parents may wish to put their babies to bed earlier than their own bedtimes, yet they don't want to wake baby up when they themselves come to bed. Some parents may like to have time to read before turning in for the night, but they don't want to keep a light on that might disturb baby's sleep. There may also be a space issue in that a small bed simply won't accommodate all of the family members who are sleeping in it.

Comfort: A parent may have his or her own body or modesty issues that make sharing a sleep space with a baby uncomfortable. Some parents may feel they cannot fully relax with a baby in bed with them. Additionally, there are some babies who don't sleep well with their parents; they become over-stimulated or hyper-alert when trying to sleep in close proximity to mom and dad.

We want to be intentional in acknowledging that all of these reasons can be legitimate causes for concern when it comes to the question of whether or not to practice co-sleeping. **And we want to make it absolutely clear that the decision whether or not to co-sleep is not a spiritual one, outside of the fact that if there is dissension between husband and wife over the issue, it is a matter to be discussed and prayed over.** There is no scriptural mandate for or against the practice, and we certainly are not prescribing it as a necessary practice of Spirit-led parenting!

Our purpose in devoting a chapter to this topic is simply to encourage those parents who might feel nudged toward co-sleeping that they can approach the issue with spiritual freedom. Each of us found sharing sleep with our babies to be very helpful and rewarding in family life, yet we both felt we had to keep it a secret from friends. Let's look at a few reasons that co-sleeping appeals to some families, as well as explore the specific resistance to co-sleeping in many Christian circles and some common questions on the subject.

What is the appeal of co-sleeping?

For some families, co-sleeping is a practical choice. Before a baby begins sleeping through the night, parents may find it more convenient to have baby close at hand to parent them back to sleep. Whether baby is in mom and dad's bed or in a bassinet close by, nighttime feedings and diaper changes can all be accomplished while barely needing to get up.

In addition to the practicality of co-sleeping, some families are drawn to the practice because it offers more time to connect with their little ones. This is especially the case for working parents who may not get to spend as much time as they would like to with their babies during the day.

Indeed, it is that sense of connectedness that many co-sleeping families treasure the most. As Grace from Pennsylvania so aptly said to us on the topic of sharing sleep space:

> *Sharing sleep space is primarily an act of emotional intimacy. The emotional safety of a shared sleep space does make it a natural place for sexual intimacy, but it is the emotional connection, not the sexual one that determines whether or not people feel safe sharing sleep. The sign that a marriage is truly on the outs is not that sex stops, but that someone starts sleeping elsewhere – like the couch. Even in a promiscuous culture of casual sex, 'spending the night' – co-sleeping – is reserved for couples that have finally made emotional commitment to each other.*
>
> *The emotional safety intrinsic to sleep sharing is why we tell secrets at sleepovers, why we bring sick and frightened kids to bed with us, and why lazy Saturday mornings are so wonderful. Sharing sleep allows families to meet a very natural and normal need with their children – nurturing an emotional bond."*

These are just a few of the reasons that families may embrace co-sleeping in one form or another.

The Marriage Bed

If co-sleeping is a practice enjoyed by families around the globe, why is there so much resistance to it in our culture, particularly in the Christian sub-culture?

The number one reason many Christian parents feel that they have to be secretive or carry guilt about co-sleeping with their babies has to do with the perception that it causes harm to marriage. Before our children were born, both of us had either consciously or subconsciously cemented the idea in our minds that the marriage bed is sacred and children must not be allowed in it. When we began to broach the topic on our blogs, we discovered we aren't the only ones who felt guilty for breaking this moral code:

> *I'm a closet co-sleeper. I don't talk about it. I admit that I even lie when it comes up.' When my family or friends ask where he sleeps, I tell them, "We have a pack-and-play set up next to our bed." That is true. The playpen is there. What I don't add is that he doesn't sleep in it. We have a crib, too, and a nursery. He doesn't sleep there, either. He sleeps in our bed, and I've not admitted it to anyone but other known co-sleepers. I'm glad we have the nighttime hours to re connect after I'm away from home at work all day. I'm just not ready to confront push-back I get in my Christian circles and come out of the closet."– Joanna, Indiana*

> *Before I had my first daughter, I had read that babies must not sleep in the parents' bed because it was unsafe, it was bad for the marriage, and they would never leave the parents' bed. I had also read that babies should not be nursed to sleep. After several months of trying everything from pacing the hall to letting her sleep in the swing, we*

decided she would move into our bed until we felt the Holy Spirit guiding us to make a different choice.

The most difficult thing for me to deal with during that time was the immense amount of guilt I felt. I had a couple of friends who co-slept, but we all felt like we were doing something wrong so rather than supporting one another's decisions we only served to deepen the guilt. I truly felt like I was failing as a wife and mother because I let my baby sleep in my bed. I am so thankful to now be free of that bondage! My newest baby, now three months old, sleeps in our bed and will continue to do so until we feel God leading us in a different direction. – Abbey, Oklahoma

Co-sleeping has definitely been taboo is some circles I am a part of. I am lucky enough to be a part of a new mamas group run by a very crunchy local baby store. But at church, a highly revered church mother figure made her opinion quite clear when she said that whatever I do, I 'had better not let that baby sleep in the bed' with me. It's hard that I can't be honest about how we function as a family. Our church is usually very open-minded, for example, I feel comfortable breastfeeding right in the pew, in mixed gender Bible studies, etc., but this is one topic that I know I can't bring up. – Lauren, Pennsylvania

We heard in these stories and the stories of others such a strong connection to our own stories: guilt about failing as both a wife and mother by allowing (and enjoying!) baby sleeping in bed. Where does this opinion of the sacredness of "the marriage bed" come from?

Unfortunately, it seems to come from a misapplication of a passage in Hebrews:

"Marriage should be honored by all, and the marriage bed kept pure, for God will judge the adulterer and all the sexually immoral." (Hebrews 13:4, NIV)

As the writer of Hebrews writes his concluding thoughts and words of encouragement to the body of Christ, he makes a point to emphasize that we should all honor marriage. Marriage is a sacred covenant between husband, wife, and God, and there is no doubt it is to be honored. In speaking on the purity of the marriage bed, it is clear from reading the second half of this verse that the writer of Hebrews is warning against harming the sanctity of marriage through adultery.

It seems to us that the term "marriage bed" here is a word picture for the entirety of intimacy within a marriage relationship. Grace from Pennsylvania said this in a conversation with us about co-sleeping:

> *The 'marriage bed' does not refer to that thing in your bedroom with a mattress. If it did, we could all have affairs, just not in our bed. Clearly, 'the marriage bed' refers to the more encompassing concept of the sexual union between husband and wife. On the floor, in a car, in a plane ... whether you are in a bed or not, it's for your spouse only.*

We want to draw out this aspect of the conversation only to encourage church culture to loosen the grip it has held on this idea of the physical marriage bed. As our friend Gretchen, mother to eight in Colorado, has said to us, **"Our lives should be our marriage bed."** Within the incredibly complex dynamic that is a marriage relationship, life offers ample ways to honor our relationships with our spouses and to pursue intimacy with them. We can't imagine that anyone teaching on the topic of marriage would suggest that the bed is the *only* place to build intimacy in marriage; it doesn't make sense, therefore, to imply bringing baby to bed will *always* cause an interruption to the marriage relationship.

If we can agree that this passage from Hebrews is not a specific indictment against co-sleeping with our children, we can allow ourselves to discuss the issue with a little more objectivity. Releasing ourselves from the idea that we *can not* explore the practice gives each couple the freedom to move on to some of the next few questions that may factor into the decision over whether co-sleeping is right for their family.

Doesn't co-sleeping interfere with sex?

One of the chief concerns we hear from those who are critical of co-sleeping is that children in the bed would naturally interfere with the sexual relationship shared between husband and wife. We have found the exact opposite to be true. Couples who co-sleep often find new and creative ways to cultivate sexual intimacy. In this phase of life, some couples appreciate the challenge to think outside the bedroom when it comes to sex.

In our chapter on keeping the spark, we cover some specific ideas on creative approaches to sex, but we want to assure you there is absolutely no reason why co-sleeping should interfere with your sex life.

What if there is disagreement on whether or not to co-sleep?

Sometimes a husband and wife will find themselves in complete agreement on co-sleeping. Both of them are either 100% in favor of practicing it, or both of them are 100% opposed to it. Even couples who at first are hesitant to share sleep with a baby may eventually find they both agree that it's the best solution for their family during this season of life.

Jason, a father of two in Oklahoma, shared this reflection in an essay on Megan's blog:

> We earnestly wanted to follow the recommendations we had read in parenting books, but the tension between "parent directed feeding" and responding to our son's clear signals that he needed to be fed was causing my wife Jenny a great deal of self-doubt and inner turmoil at an already fragile time in early parenthood. I decided to take the reins and make the call for the well-being of our family and marriage that we were going to give ourselves permission to feed our son when and where he needed to be fed.
>
> And so oftentimes, that meant responding to Eli's cries in the middle of the night. And in the best interest of getting Jenny the sleep she so desperately needed, that often meant bringing Eli back to our bed and letting him nurse himself back to sleep, while Jenny would go back to sleep herself. To be honest, I enjoyed having Eli in our bed. Granted, he wasn't the most still sleeper. We'd often wake up with a fist or foot in our nose. But there wasn't much more that I enjoyed than waking up seeing the two of them next to me and getting to steal a little time cuddling with my son. And I'm sure there are some parents who would be shocked to know that our marriage was not ruined or assigned any less significance when our son slept with us in bed.
>
> We had come to the realization in our hearts that God had purposefully given Eli to us. And with that in mind, no books, and no experts could speak with more authority on precisely how we were to raise our son in a way which

honored him as God's creation and honored his Creator back than his own parents who sought after God in making the right decisions about raising the son that He had entrusted to us.

In cases like Jason's, the issue works out wonderfully for everyone. But what happens when a couple disagrees on the issue? When spouses find themselves in disagreement on other issues such as a job change, finding a new church, or buying a home, they might practice "inaction until unity"; however, with a topic such as who is going to sleep where each night, a more immediate solution must be found!

This is when, once again, we recommend that each couple prayerfully and thoughtfully seek a solution that meets everyone's needs as closely as possible. Often, a situation like this will lend a spouse the opportunity to serve the other by setting aside their own preferences. One partner may decide that for a season of time, he or she will choose to show love by yielding to the needs of the other one. This was certainly the case with Megan's husband, Kyle, who shares this reflection on the co-sleeping season of life in their family:

> *Prior to becoming a parent, I had never heard of co-sleeping. It simply never dawned on me that a baby would do anything besides sleep in a crib. During the early days and weeks of adjusting to parenthood and facing the realization that there were many things for which I was not prepared, co-sleeping was the least of my worries.*
>
> *As Megan and I were not accustomed to having our sleep repeatedly interrupted, fatigue and desire for sleep began to rule our actions. Over the course of time we found ourselves with a co-sleeper. Because it wasn't so much of a conscious decision for us, it wasn't a topic that we gave*

much thought to and in turn, not a topic that we'd spent time discussing. We rested better and our baby girl rested better, so it just kind of happened.

As our daughter grew in size so did her sleep activity. We eventually came to the point where we were again losing sleep because second only to a wailing child, a heel to the ribcage is a magnificent sleep deterrent. It's hard for me to sleep well with a baby in bed, but I could see it made such a difference for Megan to get more sleep at night. Eventually, it worked better for Dacey to spend only a few hours of the night in our bed – and those hours were generally after four a.m. or so. It was a slow process, but eventually she began to prefer her crib to being in bed with us!

Within Kyle's thoughts on serving Megan by laying down his own desires to meet her needs, he also touched briefly on the next question.

Does co-sleeping have to be an all-or-nothing arrangement?

We'll re-emphasize that we are in no way advocating the position that co-sleeping is a necessary component of Spirit-led parenting. Those parents who do desire to try co-sleeping, however, do have many different options to prayerfully consider.

In some households, sharing sleep with baby is something that is happily practiced all night, every night. Many other families, however, find that a part-time co-sleeping system of some sort works best. As Laura shared in her story at the beginning of the chapter, Maya would sleep part of the night in her crib, but then she would often join them in bed after waking up to be fed during the night.

Megan tends to keep her babies in bed throughout the entire night until about the four-month mark when they transition to part-time co-sleeping. Time after time, we've had parents tell us that baby starts the night in the crib and then ends up with them by morning. For breastfeeding mothers especially, this tends to be an ideal solution to the fogginess that multiple nighttime feedings can cause.

Through the years, we've collected stories about what sharing sleep looks like in different families. As you'll see, the varieties of co-sleep practices are as different as the families who practice them:

> *I started off dead-set against co-sleeping because of what I had heard about it interfering with the 'marital relationship,' but that did not last long. What we have found with both of our kids that works the best for us is that we would bring them to our bed after the first time they woke up during the night. Everyone seems to sleep much deeper and longer when that happens. Now our three-and-a-half-year-old sleeps completely restfully and happily in his own bed all night and our one-year-old has been the one that has taken his spot. She starts off in her bed, but if she wakes up during the night, we simply bring her in with us and she immediately falls into a relaxed sleep. These moments won't last forever and my husband and I treasure them. We still have our evenings after the kids go to bed to do as we wish, but are so happy to not fight the 'sleep in your own bed' fight during the night as I did with my firstborn for a while. – Jennifer, Texas*

> *We co-sleep. I didn't really intend to before having children but soon after our oldest was born, I realized you do what works for your family. The extreme convenience of co-sleeping is what kept Sam in our bed for about*

the first nine months or so of his life. He had an easy transition to his bed. Now at the age of two-and-a-half he sleeps in his bed every night but if he is sick or extra fussy he sometimes ends up in our bed or more often Nathan or I end up in a makeshift bed in his floor. – Mary Ann, West Virginia

Our first was adopted, so I didn't breast feed. He also loved his bed. He never slept with us with any regularity and because my husband was able to share feeding duties, we traded off the nighttime parenting.
Then I gave birth to our second. Not only was I now breastfeeding, but I also had a baby who hated her bed. She wasn't a good sleeper anyway, but she always did better in our bed. She stayed in our bed until she was three. While we never set out to be co-sleepers, it worked for us. Everyone slept better and therefore felt better. As far as our love life goes, I think it forced us to be more creative and that's always fun. – Julie, Texas

Everyone loves to tell you why you shouldn't co-sleep with your babies. You will spoil them, or they will never leave the bed. I finally just stopped telling people about it. But for my husband and me, it has been awesome. My daughter had moments in which she would choke in her sleep, so I was not about to leave her in a crib where I couldn't respond to her if she needed me. It just felt better and safer having her right next to me. I am a working mother, so co-sleeping has been a way for us to spend a lot of time together and make up for time we missed during the day. I LOVE waking up with her. She loves to cuddle when she wakes up, and I love getting the first smiles of her day. It works for us and I love it. – Katie, Texas

I have five children and each of their sleep habits were unique as was the learning curve for my husband as I as parents. The newborns were in our room next to me in a cradle most of the time, nursed to sleep when needed and cuddled in slumber. The transition to crib came mostly from my inability to get a good night's sleep with someone squirming around. One of my daughters is like this as well and never really slept deeply unless alone.

My last child was a bit of a challenge in that she slept well during the day but woke often in the night but it wasn't necessarily to nurse because this continued even when she was older and had weaned. She found solace in her older sister's bed and she still sleeps with her often although she is now almost 11. The other sisters don't seem to sleep as well when so squished!

There was never much routine to any of it or concern over what others thought, really. Like many other families, we just found a way to make it work with each child. – Deb, Ontario

Closing Thoughts on Co-Sleeping

We share our stories and those of others not to persuade families that this is the right and necessary path for everyone, but to encourage you to feel freedom in exploring the practice as something that might be helpful, even if only for a short time. While co-sleeping itself is not an issue with a spiritual mandate, it is another area where pursuing and following the guidance of the Holy Spirit can bring peace in your parenting—whether you are led to share sleep with your baby, or not.

This tends to be a deeply personal topic that families on both sides of the issue can become quite defensive about when the matter comes up for discussion. We long to see that change; that all families could be comfortable in discussing sleeping arrangements with others, and able to be truthful without feeling ashamed.

Those sweet sleep gowns and footed pajamas are all too quickly tucked away in memory boxes as time grows our little ones into Big Kids who are so fiercely independent. Someday there will be curfews and slumber parties and all-night study sessions and eventually these babies will be teenagers who have to make space in their busy schedules for us. The nights filled with squirms, grunts, and sighs are just a whisper in the lifelong conversation that is parenting. If it's possible, if it's safe, and if it's desirable, this is a precious time to make space for the warm little bodies and sweet little sleepy sounds of the ones born from the unity cultivated in our marriage beds.

Chapter Ten

As We Stay On Track

The home that follows a less-scheduled parenting style is often portrayed as one where all structure and reason have left the building. Chaos reigns and parental authority is lost from the very beginning. What a disaster! And what a conflict for those parents who discern that following God's direction for their families means not sticking closely to a particular recommended daily plan. Are they hearing Him correctly or side-stepping a Biblical mandate? These are questions that weighed heavily on each of us in the beginning.

-Laura's Story-

By nature, I am a creature of habit. I crave predictability, and there can't be too many out-of-the-ordinary days in a row before I'm twitchy for my comfortable routine. Knowing what to expect is my security blanket, and gives me a precious sense of control. Wouldn't you know that this was something God would ask me to confront in a major way with parenthood?

While reading parenting books during my pregnancy with Maya, the part of their instructions that appealed most to me wasn't the promise of a quick return to sleep. It was the guarantee of a predictable schedule. Let's face it—I knew practically nothing about being a mother, so the prospect of stepping into an unknown world that would change my entire life was more than a little overwhelming. If I could at least get a grasp on a daily agenda that I could count on, I felt I could be more relaxed. More in control, you see.

Well, you have already read about the ways that Maya just did not get the memo about "normal" feedings and predictable sleep patterns and about how my efforts to force the issue in those areas just caused more strife and stress in our home. While I've explained that I was beginning to perceive over time that the way I was parenting Maya—responding to her frequent feeding cues, waking with her through the night, etc.— was prompted by the Spirit's leading, I have not yet pointed out how utterly out-of-character that choice was for me.

My personality and preference leaned far more toward the scheduling concept. My heart, influenced by the strong instincts I felt as I observed my baby's needs and temperament and the strong sense of God's direction, was pulling me out of my comfort zone into a different outlook—not just on parenting, but on daily life. It was one that asked me, in some new ways, to lose control.

-Megan's Story

I sat on the couch of our little apartment and thumbed through the pages of the parenting book loaned to me by someone I love and admire. In a few short weeks our baby would arrive, and I was brushing up on the guidance offered by the book. "You need to begin establishing your routine from day one," the book said[37].

---

37   Gary Ezzo, *On Becoming Babywise* (Sisters, OR: Multnomah Books, 1995) 97

In the midst of concessions such as "considering context" and admonitions to "be flexible," were instructions such as "feeding must be first, waketime second, and naptime third. Do not change that order[38] ..."

Must be.

Do not change that order.

Sunlight streamed over my shoulders onto the pages of the book and it was like heaven was opening up and saying, "Here you go. Follow these rules. You'll be fine." I nodded my head. It all made sense.

I went from being a child in my parents' home, to a university student, to a teacher. Routine, schedules, rules, and structure. These are the important things of life, right? The funny thing is that the timing of this season of life allowed me to spend the entirety of my pregnancy with Dacey with absolutely no schedule. Except for the occasional substitute teaching gig, I wasn't in the classroom at all. My husband's job required him to be gone from sunrise until long past sunset. My days were spread wide before me with no semblance of order. And I had never felt so comfortable in my own skin (well, skin tags and stretch marks, notwithstanding).

Along came baby and as I told you in chapter five, the schedules were a complete mess because of the bugaboo of sleep. The more I became obsessed and consumed with making our life look like the rosy, idyllic life of sunshine and rainbows prescribed in that parenting book, the more I felt like our days were one long, torturous psychological experiment where I was expected to cram a square peg into a round hole and my fingers and spirit were bruised from persistent failure.

---

38   Ibid

I would open my day planner and flip wistfully through the pages leading up to Dacey's birth, days when the thrill of nothing at all on the schedule motivated me to get up and explore the possibilities. But I had a baby now and it was my responsibility to keep chaos at bay, never mind the chaos in my heart and mind steeped in the tension between what I should do and what I wanted to do. Despite the fact that I was never successful at highly scheduled days, I decided to grit my teeth and try harder. Every morning, I chartered the plan for the day — down to the minute. I pushed down the part of me that was crying out for spontaneity and with pursed lips and a steely gaze, I honed in on the schedule. *Do not change that order, remember? Order.* The baby needed it, God expected it and it was up to me, I thought, to create it — *no matter how miserable it made me feel.*

* * *

The scheduling conundrum caused much confusion and frustration in our homes at first. Each of us had read enough to believe that a highly-structured day was the way to embrace God's order, yet each of us truly felt as though we were being led in a different direction. How could this be? Let's take a look at whether it is possible to parent on a Spirit-led path — even one that directs some mothers and fathers *away* from a solid schedule — while maintaining order and harmony within the household.

Proponents of a schedule-based parenting philosophy tout the importance of a parent-directed daily agenda. Implementing set times for feeding, waking, and napping, as well as an early jump on sleep-training, all help — they say — to establish solid relational dynamics with father and mother in firm control. Additionally, sticking to such a plan is promoted as the method necessary to keep God's order in the home. There are several books on the market that will provide new parents with outlines to follow as a way to accomplish these goals. And it is very true that many families find great success with these methods!

Oftentimes, however, new parents trying to mold their babies to the suggested schedule end up frustrated and discouraged, confused as to why their child won't adapt, and convinced that something must be very wrong. Such stress and uncertainty, as we experienced, can actually contribute to more *disharmony* in the home than peace and order.

Popular Arguments for Scheduling

It seems as though the argument that firm schedules are best for every baby in every Christian home is based on two main principles: establishment of parental authority and honoring God's order. Let's take a look at each of these ideas.

Authority

One of the major focal points of mainstream Christian parenting literature is the encouragement to parents that they keep a firm grip on the authority over their home and children. There is clear Biblical basis for the concept of parental authority, and we do not dispute in the least the necessity of respect, honor, and obedience given to parents by their children.

A concern that we do have, however, is that Christian infant-care literature often insists that adherence to a solid schedule for baby's day is an essential step toward maintaining parental control. There are multiple warnings given to avoid child-directed feeding patterns and hold fast to a parent-directed schedule. And there is a clear implication that failing to do so sets the stage for battles in the future over authority and discipline.

Such instruction can understandably cause great anxiety in the minds of new parents who deeply desire to honor God and His

Word with their child-rearing choices. We have heard the stories of many mothers—including stories you have already read in this book—who were determined to follow a schedule because they feared losing control of their children right out of the gate.

We have a few assertions of our own to offer in response to the theory of parent-directed scheduling with infants as a means to establishing the upper hand of control.

First, we would point out once again that a young infant is not capable of manipulating their parents or consciously seeking to usurp their authority. While toddlerhood is most definitely another story entirely, we simply do not see the physical, psychological, or spiritual basis for determining that a two-month-old baby must be trained to recognize his parents' authority by the direction of his feeding and sleeping habits.

While some parents may be led by the Spirit to follow a firm schedule, we do not believe it is God's intention that *every* mother and father take that path, or that His Word advises it implicitly as the way to raise a child who will grow to respect and honor their parents.

For Laura, one weary night in particular found me peering intently into Maya's eyes as she began another feeding. It was not a blissful, loving gaze, or peaceful mental memorization of her tiny facial features. No, what I was searching for in that moment were signs of disobedience. Something to confirm that her waking was a bad habit meant to manipulate me.

In the middle of that train of thought, however, something occurred to me. *This child cannot sit up on her own.* I remembered how earlier that day, Mark and I had decided to check the progress on this milestone by placing Maya on a blanket in a sitting position and backing our hands slowly away. Drooling and smiling, she had tipped right over, feet straight up in the air, and we had laughed aloud at the cuteness. It suddenly struck me as absurd that I would be trying to root out the manipulative aspirations of a baby who did not yet have the muscle tone to hold herself upright. I breathed a deep sigh that night, releasing myself a bit from the preoccupation with establishing proper authority and embracing the permission to just enjoy the moment.

Second, we would look toward the example of Christ, who came among us not to be served but to serve (Matthew 10:45). All authority under heaven and earth was His (Matthew 28:18), and this authority was not diminished in the slightest when He took the posture of a servant (Philippians 2:7). If the Spirit leads you to parent your baby according to a sleep or feeding schedule, you are honoring His will by doing so. But that choice alone does not make-or-break your authority.

If you are led to serve your child by adopting the practice of nighttime parenting, or if her cues signal you to feed her frequently throughout the day, you need not fear that your little one will become undisciplined or disrespectful. You will have daily opportunities as your baby grows into childhood to instill loving discipline and appropriate respect, as well as compassion, generosity, etc. That is the privilege of parenthood! With the Lord's help, we guide our children toward a right relationship with Him and with others. It is a calling that requires years of work and will weather mistakes and missteps. But we are not to fear. He knows our hearts, knows our children, and is faithful to lead us.

I'm a new Mom to a precious eight-week-old. I was pretty purposeful to not read too much about parenting styles and methods. When we encounter a bit of a struggle, I'll do some reading and go with whatever makes sense. It's worked beautifully for us. Sure there are days when I'm exhausted from long nights and lots of feedings, but being able just to dwell with her in those moments and ensure that she knows and feels I'm there and available at all times is what I'm aiming for now.

I have been thinking about God as our parent. In "infancy" as a believer, the most important thing is developing a trusting relationship with Jesus, believing and accepting His unconditional love extended to us, breaking free into the new covenant from the expectations and "schedules" of the old law. So I feel it should be with babies. Then as we mature as Christians, (and babies mature) come discipline and exercising obedience enabled because of that love relationship. -Stephanie, Ohio

Third, we feel that the push toward a parent-directed schedule can become a subtle—and surely unintended—encouragement away from *God's* direction. Both of us will admit to control-freak tendencies, and find it painfully difficult many times to turn the trajectory of our lives and plans over to the Lord's leading and guidance. The more each of us attempted to employ "parent-directed" techniques and listened to the "you must take charge!" and "let her know who is in control!" advice given by others, the more we retreated into our own wisdom (or lack thereof) rather than waiting on the wisdom of the Spirit.

Ultimately, the concept of infant scheduling linked with establishing parental authority is at best a non-issue, and at worst an unnecessary source of pressure and fear for parents being led in a different direction by the Spirit of God who knows with perfect wisdom what is right for their families. No matter how we handle the spacing of feedings or the way we parent our babies at night, our children will recognize our authority as we submit to Christ and lead our households according to His direction above our own.

God's Order

"God is a God of order." This oft-repeated statement is used in discussion topics ranging from planning a worship service, organizing ministry management and church leadership, and theological arguments over manifestations of the Holy Spirit. Scriptures such as 1 Corinthians 14:33 ("For God is not a God of disorder, but of peace." NIV) are usually cited, as well as general observations of the precise outline of the creation account in Genesis and the meticulously-detailed commands given by the Lord to the Israelites throughout Leviticus. There is no doubt that our God is in control of every facet of His vast creation, that His plans are perfect, and that He reigns with a steady hand and a desire for peace.

Within the holy order of the Lord, however, exist beautiful examples of events which would seem to our human eye to be fully chaotic. The Spirit's descent upon the believers in the upper room in Jerusalem at Pentecost, complete with tongues of fire and a sudden cacophony of various languages spoken at once, was so bewildering to observers that some believed the gathered followers of Christ to be drunk (Acts 2:13).

When the Apostle Paul and other believers were sent out to preach the gospel, they were not often given knowledge of the next day's itinerary. They simply woke up and went wherever the Spirit instructed them to go, not knowing most of the time who they would be speaking to or what the outcome would be. In fact, in some situations where they did have predetermined ideas, the Holy Spirit would not allow them to complete those plans (Acts 16:7). Instead of preaching the Gospel to people in one city as planned, they would find themselves imprisoned in another, all the while working within the will of the Lord. Giving up control, they found His peace in every circumstance.

Regardless of whether God initiates or approves of situations which may seem outwardly chaotic or whether He simply works within them, what does the end game of order appear to be when we look at the Scriptures? What is God's purpose and desire in establishing order? Our belief in examining God's Word is that God-directed order clears the path for His work to be done. He doesn't establish order merely for the sake of order, but so that His direction for organization can set the stage for successful advancement of the Kingdom.

Applying this principle to daily family life may—and should—look different from home to home. God's Word does not offer any specific examples or commands as to how an orderly day with an infant is best lived out. Within the Body of Christ, each family has a unique calling, set of responsibilities and temperaments, and way of capturing and nurturing harmony. Some families rise early each morning for chores or pre-breakfast devotionals. Others take weekends for lounging with books, board games and kicked-back times of bonding. For some households, it works best if dinner falls at 5:30 year-round, while some find that the long daylight hours of summer may push the evening meal far later a few times a week. There are families who find the most comfort and motivation in a very predictable schedule and families who find freedom and fulfillment in a looser routine.

The work of God's Kingdom in the relationships, discipleship, ministry, etc. within each home, and the type of order necessary to accomplish this work, will vary greatly. Is it okay to say that? We think so. A firm daily schedule may be the way God's order best plays out in your home during the infant-parenting days, but may be completely frustrating—and not at all His plan—for your neighbors down the street as they care for their new baby! In fact, for some, adhering to a schedule can actually squelch the Spirit's leading in their lives.

When the Schedule Becomes an Idol

Sometimes, in their best-intentioned efforts to avoid the trap that could be described as "idolatry of the newborn," parents instead fall prey to another snare: *the idolatry of the schedule*. We have noticed this schedule-as-idol issue emerge in two distinct ways in our lives and the lives of other mothers who have shared their stories with us: when the schedule *is not* working, and when it *is* working.

When Dacey was a baby, Megan obsessed over keeping detailed accounts of sleep and waking periods. While Dacey naturally fell into a feeding schedule, her sleeping habits were not conforming to the recommended charts, and Megan's quest for solutions to the discrepancy were causing her extreme amounts of stress and heartache. The more she tried to "bring God's order" to her daughter's naps and night times, the more *disharmony* the process brought to her home, marriage, and heart. Convinced that she had to enforce a sleep schedule—not because she had prayerfully determined that it was the best option for their family, but because she was under the impression that it was the only option that did not equate to failure—Megan eventually found that the elusive sleep schedule had become an idol in her life. And she is not alone in that experience.

> *Scheduling is just not part of my personality. I'm one of those 'go with the flow' types. My first daughter is just like me. But instead of listening to her needs, I decided it would be best to time her feedings and nap times and structure her day rigidly. I read books and listened to people who told me how to best manage our days and nights. I would get frustrated when she would fall asleep nursing and would try to wake her so she could fall asleep on her own by self-soothing. I wanted her to fit into a certain mold, and didn't want a spoiled baby. I spent the*

first few nights sitting by her bed listening to her cry. I was heartbroken but I truly thought I was doing what was best for her, for me, and for our family.

After a week of this, completely sleep-deprived and stressed, I picked up my baby and for the first time saw a person who had their own needs and who deserved the same respect that I gave myself. God had truly changed my heart and I owe him so much praise. Once I started responding in the way she needed, the routines just sort of fell into place. Her feedings were all over the place, but that was ok because it led to much more sleep and a much happier baby. Really listening and seeing the positive results gave me so much more confidence as a mother. – Shannon, TN

Like a typical rookie parent when our first baby was born I wanted to do everything 'by the book.' She would cry because she was hungry, but if it hadn't been the magic two-and-a-half to three hours since her last feeding I would do anything in my (exhausted) power besides what I knew she really needed ... to nurse!

When the second one came along, we did nothing by the book. With two under two, I just used my motherly instincts to care for them both. We were so much more relaxed and less stressed. I think I enjoyed our second child's infancy so much more because I wasn't worried about rules! -- Katie, Georgia

We, like so many others, were given books that promoted scheduling very young infants. The only thing it produced in our home was a lot of angst in my heart and the definite feeling that I was a failure as a mother (what a way to start out, eh?). So I felt I had to let go of it all. I did, and

I suddenly enjoyed mothering! Now with my second, I
don't even look at the clock when I feed him, I just enjoy
him. I feel that I know my child better because I am not
thinking about schedules or expectations — just him. I
think that's a lot like God with us. [The Bible] says He
delights in us and sings over us! - Shilo, Washington

But what about a schedule that is working wonderfully? What about those seasons or situations where naps are more predictable and your daily routine is fairly set? If baby is thriving and mom and dad are happy, isn't that an ideal situation? Well, yes. Most of the time. As we've said before, scheduling works wonderfully for some families from early on and most little ones eventually fall into some sort of routine as they grow. This is where it is important to watch that the success of the schedule does not become another sort of idol.

For instance, both of us found that in the older baby stages when our children had become more inclined toward a basic routine, there were moments when we elevated the importance of their self-imposed schedules over the leading of the Spirit. Rushing back from errand-running to be home by naptime makes sense most of the time. However, Laura remembers a few times when a friend who needed to talk ended up delaying the return from Mommy 'N Me, meaning Maya's naps were off-kilter and Laura moped and mumbled through a grumpy afternoon instead of praising God for allowing her to be a blessing to a sister in Christ.

Re-examining priorities and devoting yourself deeply to family life is crucial and admirable during new motherhood. Megan recalls, though, the occasional ministry opportunity missed because of her fear that it *just wouldn't work* with Dacey's routine. She found herself saying no to projects and service ventures that strongly resonated with her heart, but had the potential — she worried — to just really throw things off-kilter.

Idolatry of the schedule does what every false idol does. It replaces the Lordship of Christ in our lives. Certainly, God can and does lead some families to a highly organized daily plan. But others follow feeding and sleeping charts into turmoil and angst. If we are forcing a schedule because we are clinging to man's wisdom or fear of failure, we are not inviting his order. We are denying His sufficiency to guide us in that area of parenting and lead us by the rhythm of His Spirit to the daily flow He desires for our unique households. We are missing out on the joy He wants to give us as we care for these tiny creatures fearfully and wonderfully made in His image. We are choosing to trust in something other than the one perfect parent, who is faithful to give us all wisdom and strength when we ask (James 1:5) because of His great love.

Protecting the security of our established routines is usually a wise and healthy plan. But if we grasp the convenience of predictability so tightly that we close ourselves off to unexpected encounters with people who need to know the love of Christ, or to opportunities to serve others in our communities or church families, we must examine whether we are allowing schedule to become king rather than leaning on the Holy Spirit to guide each day.

Schedule vs. Routine

There is a difference between the concepts of *schedule* and *routine*. While a schedule tends to be a pre-timed order of the day's events and to carry connotations of rigidity, a routine is a flexible-yet-predictable flow to the day. A routine takes into account baby's needs for feeding frequency and good rest, while allowing for daily events to adjust and find new rhythm as the child grows developmentally.

You might begin anticipating the point at which baby may be ready for a regular bedtime, for instance, and set up a plan for a calming pre-sleep routine, even if nighttime feedings are still taking place. Or prayerfully work out a daily pattern that blends the infant's natural eating and napping times with the cadence of family life, allowing room for adjustment and grace.

In our experience, most children eventually thrive on some sense of routine, and find security in knowing what to expect. For this reason, even if you do not begin with a schedule in place, chances are you will fall into a routine naturally over time. Each of us found this to be true with our first children. After all of the time spent stressing over a lack of schedule with days and nights that looked nothing like the charts, there was a point at which the basic daily flow took on some steady predictability and pattern with minimal intervention on our parts.

Having that perspective when our second children arrived proved very valuable. Knowing that we didn't have to force the issue or manufacture order for the sake of order, we were far more confident in simply following God's lead and letting a routine emerge as we met the needs of the new baby along with the needs of the household.

> *Because of my personality, I was dying to get all the "answers" and "figure it all out" and especially to have a schedule. As my son got older, a routine did emerge. I would have been so much better off to try to accept that babies need us, that God made them that way, and to stop worrying that I would spoil him! - Anne, British Columbia*

It is important to reiterate that we do not offer this chapter as an argument *against* scheduling your baby's days or nights. Our intention is not to criticize one method or another, but rather to advocate for the freedom that we feel is often missing from the pages of Christian parenting resources. To schedule or not to schedule is not a black-and-white issue, and each parent or couple should therefore find peace and confidence in determining through prayer what sort of daily plan best suits their household.

Seek Him First

We would encourage each new mother and father to search their hearts and ask the Lord to reveal any motives in this decision that may be off-track. We do not advocate allowing an out-of-control climate of confusion to take over your home, nor do we encourage parental martyrdom. Neither one of those results is healthy or appropriate. A situation in which father and mother feel completely overrun, distant from one another, and spiritually drained is surely not God's intent for parenthood.

An equally inappropriate goal, however, is one of parenting merely toward convenience. Life with an infant is not simply something to be managed, but a humbling opportunity for growth, sacrifice, and servanthood. Take care in sorting these things through, and ask God to refine you and reveal more of Himself and His character in your life as He guides your days.

May our hearts and minds be ever-focused on the movement of the Spirit. And may our days be directed not by our children, not by ourselves, but by Him alone.

> *I had a moment when my son was a few months old when God spoke to me in the darkness of his room, saying, 'I am with you in your mothering,' and I did not believe it. I did not believe that God could be with me in all the little details and decisions of mothering my baby, because it seemed like it was so trivial. I know otherwise now, and*

try more and more to trust God and trust my children
and find the image of Christ in them." *- Annie, England*

Many parents can identify with Annie's reflection. We may feel completely comfortable turning to the leadership of the Spirit for major life decisions, but we feel the details of our days are too silly or trivial to bother seeking God's direction. A central truth of the Spirit-led life is that God gives to his children everything we need for every decision, for every day.

"You gave your good Spirit to instruct them. You did not withhold your manna from their mouths, and you gave them water for their thirst." *(Nehemiah 9:20,NIV)*

Finding Freedom in His Direction

For Megan, something I didn't know about myself all those years ago when I was a new mama but am very much aware of now is that it is an aspect of my personality type to resist highly-structured environments. I flourish when I am presented with a variety of possibilities, and I tend to shrivel under hard-and-fast structures.

Even more amusing to me (and I absolutely know God Himself must chuckle over this) is that Dacey, the one who caused me so much worry and angst over her schedule, is a very, very routine-driven child. Because our first attempts at scheduling were such a disaster, I have to think her inflexible tendencies come not from anything I have nurtured into her, but are instead the result of the nature in which God created her. Throughout her late infancy, on into toddlerhood and the preschool years, I've learned so much about living life in the rhythm of routine.

No one was more surprised than I was to discover that about the time she hit the six-month mark, her daytime sleep organized beautifully into those long, restful naps I had tried so hard to force in her early months. Her schedule evolved organically with very little intervention from me! Some babies find their pace quite naturally, and when they do, it's a wonderful blessing.

Because He is a loving parent, God allowed me to have a child from whom I would be grown, stretched, and challenged as I endeavored to meet her needs. My days at home with her became incredibly predictable as she grew because that was the environment in which she thrived. I didn't instill routine in our days because it was the right way to parent; I did it because God caused me to see it was the right way to parent *her*.

And because He is gracious, He also sent me a second child who is every bit as free-spirited as I am, and together we have a blast exploring and making messes and living it up in the chaos.

For Laura, I began motherhood convinced that adhering to a pre-defined schedule would bring harmony to my heart and to our household. Isn't it funny how the more you experience something like parenthood, the more you realize that you know so very little? It is truly a great thing that my God's strength is made perfect in my weakness, because He has lots of opportunities to exercise that perfection around here! Yikes.

I do know a few things, though. I know that the promises I'd read of chaos and ill-mannered, defiant children did not prove true in our household. Despite the fact that in the infant months, Mark and I were fairly un-scheduled in our parenting style, our babies grew into happy, obedient kids who thrive on the comfortable routine that emerged naturally in our home. They are flexible enough to easily roll with changes, and most definitely understand our authority in their lives. Is that because we discovered the "right way" to approach baby-care? Absolutely not. It is because, through trial and error, we somehow discovered how to fight past our own insufficiencies and anxieties to discern the direction of the Holy Spirit. By His grace alone.

Here is something else I know: if scheduling Maya's days had "worked better" for us, I would have missed out on an area of spiritual growth for which I am now profoundly thankful. My need for control is an aspect of life in which I fiercely resist dying to self. An organized, steady schedule to sail tidily through the early months of parenthood would have become a grievous idol for me, allowing me to take credit for the "success" of my orderly days, stand in judgment of those who parented differently, and find seeking God's plan for our family to be almost unnecessary.

I know for certain this is not true for everyone. But for me, personal comforts such as perceived control choke out my reliance on Christ's sufficiency. By giving me the gift of a child who needed me to care for her differently than I had planned, God saved me from myself. In teaching me to release control, He brought freedom to my life, offered me a real and tangible example of what it means to die to myself in order to serve Him and my family, and showed me the beauty found in setting my days to the rhythms of the Spirit.

Our home is harmonious when His melody leads.

Chapter Eleven

As We Have Found His Redemption

-Laura's Story-

Shortly after the morning described in our opening chapter that found me sitting in despair holding three-month-old Maya and wondering who to turn to for direction, a pivotal change began to occur in my heart. As I gradually and stubbornly decided that I was choosing to fail my own expectations and the ones of those around me, the hubbub of voices started to disappear. I couldn't hear anything anymore, and it was terrifying.

But then and only then, I began to hear God's whispers.

Offering peace and freedom from fear …

Speaking assurance that I was not a failure …

Nudging me to look at my happy, healthy little girl, my thriving marriage, and my deepening relationship with Him and know that we were on the right course … for us …

Revealing more of His Father heart, and pointing me to the ways of Christ…

Whispering the promise that His Spirit would be there to guide me …

He spoke, and confirmed the instincts He had placed in my heart from the moment He placed my daughter in my arms. He gently leads those who have young (Isaiah 40:11). He leads some mothers one way and some another because He knows and intimately understands His children. I resurfaced from the drowning and breathed deep this life-giving message: **every baby is His unique creation, every mother is His treasured child, and every family has a calling. When my heart led me to care for my daughter another way, it wasn't rebellion or failure or the beginning of ruin;** *it was Him.*

The girl who didn't want to take a step without clear direction from someone who knew better was finally learning to identify the One voice that spoke steady guidance toward His plan for our family, even when it meant a blind leap from the well-worn dust of the beaten path to an off-the-map trail of unknown twists and turns. It felt like home, and I was free. Even in those weary nights, as I fed and rocked my baby through the fatigue and frustration, there was freedom. It was sweet, it was good, and it was God.

As Maya bounded and twirled through the adventures of life as a two-year-old, we started down the path of pregnancy again, this time anticipating the birth of her little brother. I sifted through blue paint samples, washed and folded the newborn onesies, and dug out the extra nursing pads. And I left the infant-care manuals to gather dust on the bookshelf.

My due date approached, tucked into one of the most harried times of year: right between Thanksgiving and Christmas. We experienced the expected qualms about adjusting from one child to two, and pondered the mystery of how our hearts can explode anew in an expansion of love that embraces another child. We attempted to prepare ourselves for another round of sleep deprivation. And I spent time wondering what shape my breastfeeding journey would take this time around.

But I did not fear. I did not make charts or pre-set schedules. I did not fret over my marriage or build up a defensive front. I did not spend a single minute steeling myself to keep a firm resolve on my plans. In fact, I really didn't make plans. In spite of all of my addictive tendencies toward receiving instruction and holding tightly to control—I did not make plans. It still makes me shake my head in wonder.

Noah entered the world on a peaceful Sunday afternoon. Strands of white lights twinkled outside the hospital window and the snow fell softly as they brought him from the scale to my arms. The nurse asked if I wanted to try to feed him right away, and I shrugged my agreement, blissful but doubtful. Just moments later I laughed and cried simultaneously as my little boy latched on immediately. *So, You're going to go ahead and redeem it all, then, God? I should have known. Isn't that just Your way?*

Now, lest you think that the beginning months of my life as mother-of-two were all daisies and unicorns, let me assure you that there was a healthy dose of frustration and exhaustion involved. Noah had his own set of unique delights and quirks. He slept fairly well … so long as he was being cuddled. And he nursed efficiently and with slightly less frequency than his big sister had … but also developed a penchant for biting. (Ouch.)

The striking difference this time in navigating these hurdles was the sense of peace and confidence that carried me through the difficult days. While I still wrestled with fatigue and grumpiness and often found myself longing for answers, I no longer sought those solutions in the same way. I gleaned many tidbits of helpful wisdom from loved ones and other parenting resources, but I now knew to consider those things in prayer and to trust my heart. This time I knew that as I sought the wisdom of the Holy Spirit dwelling within me, I could walk in the confidence of knowing He would guide my steps.

Maya was turning three, thriving and full of budding independence. Looking back at my fears during her first few months, I smiled at the realization that the child I once worried would grow up to be clingy, disobedient, and plagued with sleep problems now skipped happily to her room each evening and slept peacefully until morning—never once giving us even a hint of a bedtime battle.

Noah was healthy, secure, and growing in every way. Mark and I were experiencing new heights in our teamwork and our love for each other. And my fear was gone. I was no longer crippled by outside expectations or desperately seeking opinions from those who knew better. In fact, I was discovering new boldness in speaking my heart, even that which went against the grain. And it was all because I now knew what it was like to have my best-laid plans foiled by a God who knew He had something far better for my life.

I knew that having children would change everything. What I didn't know was how He would change me.

Sitting once more in the early morning hours, as the first rays of light began to peek through the windows, I found myself on the same couch, watching the same clock march steadily toward morning. Noah dozed and I leaned my head back, resting my eyes just a few minutes longer. It had been an interrupted night, and I had a full day ahead. An energetic toddler would be yawning awake and calling me at any moment. There would be breakfast to make and diapers to change. I was tired. But it was okay.

I had weathered the journey of learning to discern the whispers of the Spirit and choosing to follow. It hadn't been easy. It ripped away the comfort of knowing I was taking the popular path. It stripped me of the security I'd long found in relying on the opinions of others. It cost me predictability, convenience, sleep, time, and the fulfillment of my own plans and desires.

Was it worth the cost?

Soaking in the full-circle beauty of the moment, I knew that the answer was a clear and breathtaking *yes*.

-Megan's Story-

"Can I go on stage now, Mommy?"

I remember looking down into Dacey's three-year-old eyes, crinkled at the corners the way mine do when I smile. She was beaming and bouncing, ready to join her Vacation Bible School friends on stage in front of the entire church. I nodded yes and she was off, a blur of long brown hair and pink sandals and arms and legs that were undeniably more child than baby.

I watched her sing and do her best with the song motions, full of confidence and joy. I feel like God and I had a secret, private moment there in the church pew as I watched my oldest daughter on stage. Warmth spread over me as I thought back on the baby I was so terrified I would ruin. Though years had passed since I had collapsed against her bedroom door, sobbing under the crushing weight of fear and failure, the emotions of those memories were never far from the surface.

Before my eyes, Dacey had grown into an incredible child—smart, funny, confident, and wildly independent. She was healthy and helpful, curious and wise. Daily I could envision her conquering any study under the sun: science, poetry, art. She could do anything. She slept peacefully in her own bed all night, every night. She didn't even shed a tear when it was time for her to move out of the crib and into a Big Girl bed to make way for her baby sister.

I pulled her baby sister, our Aliza Joy, close and pointed to her big sister on stage. AJ is my redemption child, the one whom I parented solely by the guidance of Spirit-fueled maternal instinct and the rhythms of God's grace. Though certainly there were moments when I was parenting both a new baby and a toddler that I felt worn thin and stretched beyond what I thought I could bear, I had long since learned that leaning into my weakness brought me closer to Christ.

All of this makes it that much harder to confess this to you: remember back in Chapter One when I told you that the person who first gave me a parenting book also shared some advice, words that I chose to ignore? The advice from that person whom I love and respect was this:

> *Never forget that you have the Holy Spirit who will help you know what to do.*

I could laugh and cry even now as I write that. I feel like Dorothy staring at the ruby slippers that would have taken her home, the ones she had been wearing all along. But like Dorothy, I also had to follow my own path, a journey to help me learn that I could trust God in everything in life, even, and especially, parenting. I had become convinced by the systems of this world that orderly schedules and exerting control were the keys to healthy and productive living.

I was uncomfortable with the freedom of following the Spirit because I had never really lived abandoned to the Spirit. It wasn't until I was thrown into the wilds of parenting that I realized I had tamed God's Voice to a whisper. It wasn't until my carefully-constructed plans crumbled around me the moment I first held my baby in my arms that I finally awakened to the reality that all of my plans were always only an illusion of control.

I could imagine God giving me a wink as together we watched Dacey on that church stage. I could feel Him whisper in my spirit, *"So you can trust Me with her after all, don't you think?"* I could envision leaning into His Fatherly embrace, now fully aware that I had never once been alone on this parenting path.

Perhaps someday I'll be able to think back on my earliest days and weeks of parenting without flinching and sighing with regret. As much as I wish I could have those days to live over again, to replace the voice of the experts with words of prayer, to celebrate what *was* instead of mourning what *was not*, and to surrender gently rather than stubbornly resist, there still is part of me that is filled with gratitude for the journey. Without the pain, anguish, tears, and heartache, I never could have understood the depths of mercy and the richness of grace that is to be found in the Spirit-led life. I wouldn't trade the depth of this life for the shallows of the life I knew before, not for all the uninterrupted nights of sleep in the world.

Afterword

We want to offer our deepest gratitude to each of you who have chosen to bring our words into your lives. It is no small thing to trust the guidance of someone else when it comes to parenting, and we are truly honored to have come alongside you on this journey.

Our hope is that all we have shared in these pages will direct you back — *always and only* — to the LORD our God. We believe that before you were even born, God chose *this* unique moment in time to invite you into parenthood. Long before you realized it, He was already equipping and preparing you for the powerful, life-changing, soul-shaping work of parenting.

Oh, the tears we shed in our earliest days, weeks, and months as mothers. Those dark days were marked with bitter despair and painful hopelessness. We could barely imagine surviving that season of life, let alone one day sharing a message of hope and redemption with other new parents. For two women who ruefully slammed closed other parenting books and collapsed into puddles of tears, the thought of having our names associated with a book on parenting is terrifying and humbling.

Friend, you are so dearly, dearly loved by us. We have thought about you and prayed for you with every word that we labored over as this book began to take shape. We believe in you, and we know that God will reveal Himself to you in a mighty way as you seek His heart in all areas of parenting your children.

Our encouragement to you is to pray, pray, and pray some more. It would be so much easier (*wouldn't it?*) if God had included a short but very specific book in the Bible with black-and-white instructions on all things parenting. But rather than burdening us with more law, He had to have known His gracious offer of freedom would woo us ever closer to Him.

We have included a devotional section in the Appendix, as well as a set of questions for group discussion, and a list of resources that we hope will be of help to you as you continue on the path of Spirit-Led Parenting.

Appendix

The first year with your baby, no matter your parenting style, is both amazing and exhausting. Our deepest desire with the message of this book is to point new parents more deeply into the very heart of God, pursuing Him above all else and drawing encouragement from His Word. It would be an honor to spend some time in the Scriptures with you, soaking in the stunning beauty of God's promises. What we have collected is just a meager sampling of the wealth of truth and assurance available at all times to each of us as followers of Christ.

We encourage you to pray these Scriptures over your child, your marriage, and your home. Pray with your spouse, or on your own. Pray as you wake to start a new day of parenting, and during those weary nighttime feedings. We also know that when life is tiring and confusing, it is often difficult to find words. For those who could use some refreshment and inspiration, we have provided some sample prayers.

May each of us be changed and strengthened in Him again and again as we meditate on God's living, active, and eternal Word.

God the Father

Verses to Read: Romans 8:15-16, Isaiah 40:11, Psalm 139:1-16

Dear Heavenly Father,

My heart rejoices at the knowledge of how intimately You know me: my thoughts, my words, my ways. You knew every day of my life before You gave me breath. More than simply Your creation, You call me your child, my adoption affirmed by Your Spirit.

I praise You, I thank You, and I rest deeply in the certainty that just as You know me perfectly and completely, You know my baby in the same way. You love this child more than I could ever imagine or comprehend, delighting in [his/her] uniqueness and holding secure a full understanding of each and every need [he/she] will ever have. Each day that I parent this little one, help me to trust fully in Your gentle guidance, following Your direction as You shepherd me through uncertainties and difficult decisions. I pray that Your hand would be upon me always, hemming me in behind and before, keeping me safely in the center of Your will.

In Jesus' Name, Amen

Strength and Endurance

Verses to Read: Psalm 18:28, 2 Thessalonians 2:16-17, Psalm 73:25-26, Psalm 63:6-8, Ephesians 3:16-17

Almighty God,

In these days of incredible joy mixed with overwhelming exhaustion, I am in desperate need of Your strength. Thank You for the assurance of Your presence with me through restless nights and sleepy days. Though I am so weak in my humanity, in You I have everything I need. Help me resist the temptation to lean on my own power, and lead me by Your Spirit to a place of deep trust, so that my heart can be a dwelling place for Christ, rooted and strengthened in Your love.

Thank You for upholding me and encouraging my heart, caring so faithfully for me as I care for the little one You have placed in my arms.

In Jesus' Name, Amen

Patience and Perspective

Verses to Read: Philippians 4:8, Psalm 16:7-8, Colossians 3:12

Heavenly Father,

Within this incredible blessing of parenthood, I often find myself frazzled and frustrated. The responsibilities of each day seem to stretch endlessly before me and sometimes it feels as though nothing is going "right." Forgive me, Lord, for my frequent grumbling and complaints. I pray that You would soften the bristled areas of my heart and transform my attitude, opening my eyes to see these moments of setback through Your eyes. I pray that by Your Spirit, my words and actions toward my family would exude patience and my thoughts would be fixed upon things excellent and praiseworthy.

As You guide me through each day and reveal Your truth to me in the hours of the night, help me to bless You and my family by faithfully putting on the garments of compassion and patience, even and especially when it is difficult. I thank You for the precious knowledge that I am deeply and dearly loved, and that You are with me always.

In Jesus' Name, Amen

Wisdom and Counsel

Verses to Read: James 1:5, Psalm 32:8, 1 Corinthians 2:10-12, Romans 12:1-2, Psalm 143:10, John 14:15-17

Lord of all Lords,

You know my heart so intimately and perfectly, and how deeply I desire to please You in my parenting. You are familiar with the time spent reading and researching, worrying and wondering, wanting so much to have all the right answers. Thank you for the wise counsel of people in my life. Forgive me, though, for the times I have neglected to seek Your wisdom or have ranked it lower in my mind than the wisdom of man or my own predetermined notions.

Teach me to walk by the wisdom and counsel of the Spirit, who searches all things, is always present, and leads me into all truth. Renew my mind so that I may discern Your perfect will for my family. I pray that You would pour out Your wisdom into my life as a mother, as I am so lacking and You are so faithful. Thank You for Your promise to guide me along the best path, with me in every step.

In Jesus' Name, Amen

Grace and Hope

Verses to Read: 2 Corinthians 12:9, Romans 15:1, 2 Corinthians 9:8, Lamentations 3:22-23

God of Hope,

I praise You for the abounding grace that is powerfully sufficient to overcome my every frailty! In the moments of mothering where I feel entirely insufficient, remind me anew of the promise of this grace, and that in You, I truly have everything I need to abound in the good work of caring for my child. I pray that the Holy Spirit would lead me daily to lay my weaknesses before You, causing the power of Christ to rest on me in their place, and allowing me to overflow with hope as I trust in Him.

Thank You, my God, for Your faithful, ceaseless love! I hold fast to Your mercies, marvelously new every bleary-eyed morning. Your sufficient grace is the hope ever before me as I walk the road of parenting.

In Jesus' Name, Amen

Comfort and Rest

Verses to Read: 2 Corinthians 1:3-4, Isaiah 40:28-29, Psalm 91:1-2, Matthew 11:28-30

God of all Comfort,

On those days when my soul is weary and all I can see are my parenting failures, I thank You that I can fall into the arms of the Father of Compassion. My human understanding is so limited, but Yours is greater than I can comprehend. My troubles seem so heavy in this moment, but You never grow weary, and Jesus beckons me to come. Lord, give me rest for my soul in Your shadow and shelter.

As You comfort me in my times of trouble, equip me to be a comfort to others, serving my family, nurturing my child by the power of Your Spirit, and loving with tenderness, compassion, and selflessness. I pray that You would lead me into moments of rest, refreshing me again for the work set before me.

In Jesus' Name, Amen

Peace and Joy

Verses to Read: Philippians 4:6-7, 1 Peter 5:7, Psalm 42:8, Psalm 118:24

Dear Lord,

I confess to You that although I know You did not give me a spirit of fear, I far too often fall prey to fear and anxieties that shake my heart and displace my trust in You. I fret over parenting decisions and worry endlessly about my baby's present and future needs. Forgive me, Father, for allowing these fears to pervade my life. Help me to take each thought captive and make it obedient to Christ, and to take my every need before You in prayer. Guard my heart and my mind in Christ Jesus with your transcendent peace.

Father, remind me afresh each morning of the joyous gift of parenthood. As You pour Your love over me, may my own heart overflow with love and praise to You, and with a pure, fearless love for my child. In those nights when the waking hours grow long, cast out my worries and replace them with songs of praise and prayers to You, the One who gives me life. I will rejoice in each day You have made, and be glad in what You have done.

In Jesus' Name, Amen

A Servant's Heart

Verses to Read: Mark 10:45, Philippians 2:1-11, Galatians 2:20, Hebrews 13:15-16

Father God,

Thank you for the beautiful and humbling example of servanthood set before me by Christ Jesus, my Lord and Savior. Caring for an infant is one of the most profound opportunities I will ever have to follow that lead and die to my own plans and selfish desires. I pray that you who began this work in me would bring it to completion, guiding me ever deeper into a life that reflects Jesus.

As I sit up at night, persevere through tearful feedings, change countless tiny clothes and diapers and work through unending laundry piles, may I learn to count it all as reason for praise and a path toward truer communion with Christ. I pray that You would mold my attitude to match that of my Savior, that I would bring glory to Your name.

In Jesus' Name, Amen

Life by the Spirit

Verses to Read: Job 32:8, Romans 8:11, Romans 8:26-27, 2 Corinthians 3:17, Galatians 5:22-25

Gracious Lord,

I praise Your name for the astounding gift of your Spirit within me, the very same Spirit who raised my Savior from the dead! My mind cannot fully comprehend this truth, nor can my heart contain the gratitude and wonder it stirs within me. I pray that You would constantly cultivate the fruit of the Holy Spirit in my life and in my parenting, and that You would help me to live not by my flesh but by His breath alone.

Thank you also for the intercession of the Spirit, lifting my life before You in my times of weakness. Remove from my heart the shackles of fear and human expectations and open my eyes to the beauty of the freedom found wherever the Spirit leads!

In Jesus' Name, Amen

Questions for Group Discussion

Chapter One: As We Began

1. Are there parts of Megan or Laura's stories that you relate with personally?

2. If you are already a parent, what expectations of yourself or your baby did you build in your mind during pregnancy? How did reality differ from those expectations?

Chapter Two: As We Confess Our Fears

1. Have you experienced any of the initial fears (fear of chaos, fear of judgment from others, fear of failure) or subsequent fears (What is wrong? What will people say? What does God think?) discussed in this chapter, either while pregnant or in the early months of parenthood? Are you able to identify the source(s) of these fears?

2. In what ways have you noticed your parenting-related fears impacting your life, relationships, or walk with God?

Chapter Three: As We Pursue Another Way

1. What appeals to you about the idea of seeking God's individual leading for your family as you care for your baby? What about this approach makes you feel uncomfortable?

2. In what ways have you leaned on the example of God the Father, the call of God the Son, and the power of God the Spirit in your parenting? What has held you back from fully embracing these gifts?

3. Which aspects of freedom in parenting appeal most to you as you read this chapter?

4. Talk about the difficulty of dying to self, and how you have seen spiritual growth in other areas of your life as you have

laid down your own desires and expectations to pursue the way of Christ. How might God desire to use the season of parenting an infant to deepen your walk with Him?

Chapter Four: As We Feed Them

1. What factors have impacted your feeding choices with your baby/babies?

2. What difficulties did you encounter, whether with breastfeeding or bottle feeding? Did you experience physical difficulties? Personal disappointment? Judgment from others?

3. If any aspect of infant-feeding has been painful for you, what has been helpful in the healing process? Are there elements of those experiences that are still difficult to deal with?

4. Why do you think feeding choices are such contentious subjects between parents? What could you do to help foster an environment of encouragement within your circles of friends, supporting them as they nourish their little ones?

Chapter Five: As They Sleep

1. What were the most common questions you received from family and friends about how your new baby was sleeping? How did you respond?

2. Tell about a time when you felt God speaking to you in the middle of the night.

3. What would you tell a new parent about how to approach the areas of sleep and sleeplessness? What worked best for you on a spiritual level? What about on a physical level?

Chapter Six: As We Parent Together

1. What fears did you or do you have about how parenting affects marriage?

2. In what ways have you seen evidence of the false dichotomy that insists that a spouse must choose to nurture the children *or* the marriage? In what ways have you seen support for a more holistic view of marriage in the midst of parenting young children?

3. How has parenting challenged your marriage? How has the season of parenting allowed you and your spouse to grow closer together?

Chapter Seven: As We Keep the Spark

1. Was, or is, the idea of a decline in physical intimacy something you fear/feared upon entering parenthood? If so, where did that fear come from?

2. How comfortable are you discussing this subject with your spouse? What are some small steps you could take to begin improving communication about this aspect of your relationship?

3. Is this an area of your marriage that you typically pray over? Why or why not? Are there attitudes you have held about intimacy with your spouse that God may be asking you to change?

Chapter Eight: As We Encourage the Connection

1. Do you feel there are remnants of the "don't spoil the baby!" perspective in your circle of friends or family? What about in your faith community?

2. On a practical level, how did you, or will you, foster a healthy connection with your child(ren) during infancy?

3. In what ways has parenting a baby strengthened your relationship and connection with God?

Chapter Nine: As They Sleep ... Where?

1. Is co-sleeping a taboo topic or openly accepted in your circle of friends? How is it viewed in your faith community?

2. Did your views on co-sleeping change after you had children?

3. Did you and your spouse agree on the topic of co-sleeping? If not, how did you seek to find a workable compromise?

Chapter Ten: As We Stay On Track

1. Do you naturally tend to thrive within highly-organized or more laid-back environments? How have those personal tendencies impacted the way you approach, or plan to approach, days and nights with a new baby?

2. How has the idea of parental authority affected your views on how to plan your baby's days?

3. Talk about what God's order means to you, and what it looks like – or could look like – in your individual homes as you raise your children.

4. Do you identify with Laura or Megan's personality or experiences? Does structure become a safety net or source of frustration for you? How might God desire to stretch or grow you in these areas as you parent?

Chapter Eleven: As We Have Found His Redemption

1. In what ways have you seen God redeem painful experiences from the season of parenting a new baby? Do you have stories to share about how He led you to freedom?

2. Are there still parts of your parenting journey that you hope will be redeemed one day? How can others pray for you

Questions for Group Discussion 227

and encourage you as you seek the Lord's healing in those areas?

3. If you have not yet entered parenthood, what do you take away from the stories shared by Megan, Laura, and others that you feel will be helpful as you start down the unfamiliar road of parenting?

4. What are some ways in which you plan to embrace Spirit-led parenting in your life and in your home?

Resources

Breastfeeding

Kellymom.com

Best for Babes: http://www.bestforbabes.org/

Kathleen Huggins, *The Nursing Mother's Companion*

Babywearing

The Babywearer: http://www.thebabywearer.com

Mothering Community - Babywearing Resources page: http://www.mothering.com/community/a/babywearing-resources

Sleep/Co-sleep

The No-Cry Sleep Solution, Elizabeth Pantley

Kellymom.com: The Family Bed http://www.kellymom.com/parenting/sleep/familybed.html

Mother-Baby Sleep Lab at Notre Dame (Dr. James McKenna's research website): http://cosleeping.nd.edu/

Infant development

Zero to Three – National Center for Infants, Toddlers, and Families: http://zttcfn.pub30.convio.net/

Better Brains for Babies: http://www.bbbgeorgia.org/index.php

Postpartum depression

Postpartum Progress: http://www.postpartumprogress.com

Essay by Nish Weiseth, on overcoming PPD through counseling:

http://www.theoutdoorwife.com/2010/03/inked-part-4.html

Essay by Allison Olfelt on overcoming PPD with medication and counseling:

http://omyfamilyblog.com/2010/08/by-all-means-let-him-work-miracles/

Books to guide beyond infancy

Grace-Based Parenting, Tim Kimmel

Families Where Grace is in Place, Jeff Van Vonderen

Biblical Parenting, Crystal Lutton

Heartfelt Discipline, Clay Clarkson

The Mission of Motherhood, Sally Clarkson

The Ministry of Motherhood, Sally Clarkson

Where to find us

Laura – In the Backyard blog: http://www.inthebackyard.net/

Megan – SortaCrunchy blog: http://www.sortacrunchy.net/